HIPPO BOOKS

D1614465

Airliners

by John W. R. Taylor

completely revised and updated

HAMLYN
LONDON · NEW YORK · SYDNEY · TORONTO

ANTONOV An-10A and An-12 (Russia)

First Flight (An-10): **March 1957**

AIRFRAME (An-10)

High unswept wings, with slight anhedral on outer panels. Unswept tail surfaces, with large dorsal fin and small ventral fins under rear fuselage. Conventional control surfaces and double-slotted Fowler flaps. Tricycle undercarriage with twin nose-wheels. Main units are four-wheel bogies which retract into long blister fairings on the sides of the fuselage.

AIRFRAME (An-12)

Differs from An-10 in having a more upswept rear fuselage with a loading ramp built into the undersurface.

ENGINES

Four Ivchenko AI-20K turboprops, each rated at 4,000 h.p. and driving four-blade reversible-pitch airscrews. Fuel tanks with capacity of 3,058 gal. in wings.

PAYLOAD

Crew of four or five. An-10A has seats in pressurised cabin for 100–130 passengers. An-12 has unpressurised main freight hold, with small pressurised cabin for 14 passengers between hold and flight deck.

DIMENSIONS

Wing span (An-10A): 124' 8". *Length (An-10A):* 111' 6½"; *(An-12):* 108' 3". *Wing area (both):* 1,292 sq. ft.

WEIGHT (An-10A)

Max. take-off weight: 121,500 lb.

PERFORMANCE (An-10A)

Max. cruising speed: 444 m.p.h.
Service ceiling: 33,500'.
Take-off run: 2,300'–2,625'.
Typical range: 745 miles at 390 m.p.h. at 33,000' with full payload.

The An-10 was designed by Oleg Antonov mainly for operation on the internal services of Russia's national airline, Aeroflot. The first version to enter service, in July 1959, was the An-10 with 84 seats. It was followed in February 1960 by the An-10A, as described above, with a 6 ft. 7 in. longer fuselage and seats for 100 passengers. This is now the main version used by Aeroflot and is capable of operating into quite small aerodromes. Alternative cabin layouts accommodate 120 or 130 passengers. The An-12 is a heavy freight version. It is in service with the airlines and air forces of the Soviet Union and several of its allies.

ANTONOV An–14 PCHELKA (Russia)

First Flight: **March 15, 1958**

AIRFRAME

High unswept wings, with single bracing strut each side. Double-slotted flaps and slotted ailerons. Unswept tail surfaces, with twin rectangular fins and rudders at tips of dihedral tailplane. Pod-and-boom fuselage, with clam-shell rear doors which form underside of upswept rear fuselage. Non-retractable tricycle undercarriage, with single wheel on each unit.

ENGINES

Two Ivchenko AI–14RF nine-cylinder radial engines, each rated at 300 h.p. and driving a three-blade airscrew.

PAYLOAD

Pilot and one passenger side-by-side on flight deck. Six passengers in pairs in main cabin, with provision for seventh seat. Agricultural version carries 220-gallon chemical tank in cabin.

DIMENSIONS

Wing span: 72' 2".   *Length:* 37' 1½".
Height: 15' 2½".   *Wing area:* 441 sq. ft.

WEIGHTS

Max. payload: 1,590 lb.
Max. take-off weight: 7,935 lb.

PERFORMANCE

Max. cruising speed: 118 m.p.h.
Take-off run: 295'.
Typical range: 423 miles at 109 m.p.h. with 1,390-lb. payload.

When designing the Pchelka (Little Bee), Oleg Antonov set out to produce a simple little aeroplane that could be flown by day or night, even in bad weather, by pilots of average skill. It can be used for passenger or freight transport in areas with no proper aerodromes. An executive version is offered, with de luxe seating for five passengers; the ambulance model carries six stretchers and an attendant; and one of the prototypes (which had 260 h.p. AI–14R engines) has been seen with a chemical tank in the cabin and spray-bars running under the wings, down the bracing struts and under the fuselage. The An–14 is used by Aeroflot and the air forces of Russia and its allies, including East Germany.

ANTONOV An–24V Srs. II (Russia)

First Flight (An–24 Prototype): **April 1960**

AIRFRAME

High unswept wings, with slight anhedral on outer panels. Slightly swept tail surfaces, with dihedral on tailplane and with both dorsal and ventral fins. Conventional control surfaces and double-slotted Fowler type trailing-edge flaps. Tricycle undercarriage with twin wheels on each unit. All wheels retract forward, main units into engine nacelles.

ENGINES

Two Ivchenko AI–24A turboprops, each rated at 2,550 h.p. and driving a four-blade airscrew. Fuel tanks with standard capacity of 1,220 gal. in wings.

PAYLOAD

Crew of two or three on flight deck. Seats in pressurised cabin for 44–50 passengers, four-abreast, with galley, cloakroom, toilets, luggage and freight compartments. Mixed passenger-freight and all-freight versions are available.

DIMENSIONS

Wing span: 95′ 9½″.   *Length:* 77′ 2½″.
Height: 27′ 3½″.   *Wing area:* 807 sq. ft.

WEIGHTS

Basic operating weight: 29,320 lb.
Max. take-off weight: 46,300 lb.

PERFORMANCE

Max. speed: 310 m.p.h.
Service ceiling: 27,560′.
Take-off run: 1,970′.
Typical range: 341 miles at 280 m.p.h. at 20,000′ with full payload.

Developed to replace the Il–14 and other piston-engined types in service with Aeroflot, this elegant little twin-turboprop transport is Russia's counterpart of the Handley Page Herald and Fokker Friendship.

The An–24 entered service with Aeroflot in September 1963 and has been exported to more than ten foreign countries. The An–24RV differs in having a 1,985 lb.s.t. turbojet in the rear of the starboard nacelle as a take-off booster. The An–24T freighter has a belly hatch under the rear fuselage and folding passenger seats. A new version of it has a rear loading ramp and 2,820 h.p. AI–24T engines.

AVIATION TRADERS ATL.98 CARVAIR (Great Britain)
First Flight: **June 21, 1961**

AIRFRAME
Basically similar to that of Douglas DC-4 (see page 58). New and very bulbous front fuselage enables the flight deck to be located above the main cabin, with a large sideways-hinged loading door for vehicles in the nose. The fin and rudder are also larger.

ENGINES
Four Pratt & Whitney R-2000-7M2 fourteen-cylinder two-row radial engines, each rated at 1,450 h.p. and driving a three-blade airscrew. Fuel tanks with total capacity of 2,390 or 2,993 gal. in wings.

PAYLOAD
Crew of two or three on flight deck. Normal payload is five motor-cars and 22 passengers, with the passenger cabin at the rear. Alternatively, seats for 85 passengers can be installed.

DIMENSIONS
Wing span: 117′ 6″.   *Length:* 102′ 7″.
Height: 29′ 10″.   *Wing area:* 1,462 sq. ft.

WEIGHTS
Empty: 41,365 lb.
Max. take-off weight: 73,800 lb.

PERFORMANCE
Max. speed: 250 m.p.h.
Service ceiling: 18,700′.
Take-off run: 3,400′.
Typical range: 2,300 miles at 204 m.p.h. at 10,000′ with full payload.

Despite its unusual appearance, the Carvair is simply a Douglas DC-4 Skymaster with a new nose and slightly bigger tail. Its name (short for car-via-air) gives a clue to its main job, for it was produced by Aviation Traders for use on the car ferry services of British Air Ferries. By putting the flight crew above the cabin, the designers have made it possible to load motor-cars straight into the 80-ft. long cabin through a large nose-door, with surprisingly little effect on handling qualities or performance. Carvairs are also in service with Eastern Provincial (Canada), Aviaco (Spain), Compagnie Air Transport (France) and Ansett-ANA (Australia).

BAC ONE-ELEVEN SERIES 200 (Great Britain)

First Flight: **August 20, 1963**

AIRFRAME

Low wings, swept back at 20°. Sweptback tail surfaces, with variable-incidence tailplane mounted at tip of fin. Each wing fitted with aileron, two spoiler-airbrakes and Fowler flaps. Engines mounted on each side of rear fuselage. Tricycle undercarriage with twin wheels on each unit. Nose-wheels retract forward, main wheels inward.

ENGINES

Two Rolls-Royce Spey–25 Mk. 506 turbofans each rated at 10,330 lb.s.t. Fuel tanks in wings and centre-section with capacity of 2,240 or 3,085 gal.

PAYLOAD

Crew of two on flight deck. Seats in pressurised cabin for up to 89 passengers, with first-class seats four-abreast and tourist-class five-abreast. Galley and coat space aft of flight deck. Toilet at rear of main cabin. Air-stair doors under rear fuselage and at front of cabin. Two underfloor cargo holds.

DIMENSIONS

Wing span: 88′ 6″.   *Length:* 93′ 6″.
Height: 24′ 6″.   *Wing area:* 1,003 sq. ft.

WEIGHTS

Basic operating weight: 46,405 lb.
Max. take-off weight: 79,000 lb.

PERFORMANCE

Max. cruising speed: 548 m.p.h.
Max. cruising height: 35,000′.
Take-off run: 6,500′.
Typical range: 875 miles at 507 m.p.h. at 25,000′ with full payload.

The BAC One-Eleven is Britain's jet successor to the turboprop Viscount and a total of **188 had been ordered by early 1970**, over one-third of them by U.S. operators. The basic Series 200 is seen in the insignia of companies like B.U.A. (Britain), Aer Lingus (Ireland) and Braniff and Mohawk (U.S.A.). The widely-used Series 300 and 400 have 11,400 lb. s.t. Spey 511s and higher weights. Users of the 97/119-passenger Series 500, with greater span and length, include B.E.A. The latest Series 475 combines the 93′ 6″ wings of the Series 500 with the original shorter fuselage.

BAC (VICKERS) SUPER VC10 (Great Britain)

First Flight (VC10): **June 29, 1962**

AIRFRAME

Low wings, swept back at 32° 30'. Swept-back tail surfaces, with variable-incidence tailplane mounted at tip of fin. Each wing fitted with two-section ailerons, three spoilers, Fowler flaps and leading-edge slats. Engines mounted in lateral pairs on each side of rear fuselage. Tricycle undercarriage, with twin nose-wheels and main four-wheel bogies. Nose-wheels retract forward, main wheels inward.

ENGINES

Four Rolls-Royce Conway RCo. 43 turbofans, each rated at 21,800 lb.s.t. Fuel tanks in wings and tail fin, with capacity of 19,365 gal.

PAYLOAD

Crew of three or four on flight deck. Seats in pressurised cabin for up to 174 passengers. Two underfloor cargo holds, with total capacity of 1,842 cu. ft.

DIMENSIONS

Wing span: 146' 2".   *Length:* 171' 8".
Height: 39' 6".   *Wing area:* 2,851 sq. ft.

WEIGHTS

Basic operating weight: 158,594 lb.
Max. take-off weight: 335,000 lb.

PERFORMANCE

Max. cruising speed: 581 m.p.h.
Service ceiling: 42,000'.
Typical range: 4,720 miles at 550 m.p.h. at 38,000' with full payload.

The VC10 and its 13-ft. longer development, the Super VC10, were Britain's 'prestige' airliners of the mid-1960s. They had to compete with advanced versions of the well-established Boeing 707 and Douglas DC-8; but introduced a number of 'second generation' features which make them highly efficient. The rear engine installation leaves the wing entirely free of engine mountings and intakes. This, together with high-lift devices, gives the VC10 and Super VC10 an excellent take-off performance from comparatively small airports.

B.O.A.C. has 12 VC10s which have 20,370 lb.s.t. Conway RCo. 42 engines and can carry up to 151 passengers, and 17 Super VC10s. Other orders for the VC10 came from Ghana Airways, British United Airways and the R.A.F. East African Airways has five Super VC10s.

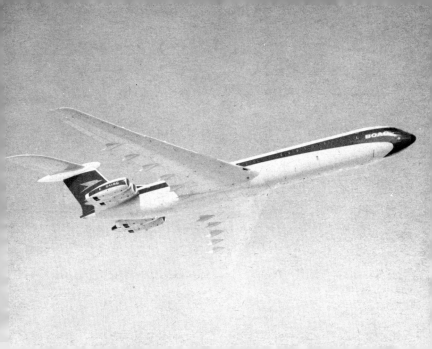

BAC/AEROSPATIALE CONCORDE (Great Britain/France)

First Flight: **March 2, 1969**

AIRFRAME

Low-set wings of delta shape with 'ogee' curved leading-edges, and three elevons on trailing-edge of each wing. Square-cut fin and rudder. No tailplane. Engines mounted in large ducts under wings. Tricycle undercarriage, with twin nose-wheels and main four-wheel bogies. Nose wheels retract forward, main units inward.

ENGINES

Four Rolls-Royce/SNECMA Olympus 593 turbojets, each rated initially at 38,050 lb.s.t. with reheat. Fuel tanks in wings and fuselage, with total capacity of 25,800 gal.

PAYLOAD

Crew of three on flight deck. Seats for up to 128 passengers four-abreast in pressurised cabin with galleys and toilets. Freight holds under floor and in rear fuselage.

DIMENSIONS

Wing span: 84'.   *Length:* 203' 8¾".
Height: 39' 10¼".   *Wing area:* 3,856 sq. ft.

WEIGHTS

Basic operating weight: 169,000 lb.
Max. take-off weight: 385,000 lb.

PERFORMANCE

Max. cruising speed: 1,450 m.p.h. at 50,000–62,000'.
Service ceiling: 65,000'.
Take-off distance to 35': 9,850'.
Typical range: 4,020 miles at 1,350 m.p.h. with full payload.

Under development as a joint Anglo-French project, the Concorde was the first supersonic airliner to fly in the Western world. It has a delta wing with curved 'wine-glass' shape leading-edges, giving what is called an 'ogee' wing planform. By limiting the top speed to just over twice the speed of sound, it has been possible to build the Concorde mainly of conventional light alloys. Higher speeds would require an all-steel airframe. A total of 74 Concordes had been ordered by the spring of 1970, including eight each for B.O.A.C., Air France and Pan American World Airways.

The fuselage nose can be drooped to improve the pilot's view during take-off and landing. The Concorde is expected to be ready for service by 1973.

BEECHCRAFT 99 (U.S.A.)

First Flight: **July 1966**

AIRFRAME

Low unswept wings. Swept tail surfaces, with small dorsal and ventral fins. Conventional control surfaces and slotted flaps. Tricycle undercarriage, with rearward-retracting nose-wheel and twin-wheel main units which retract forward into engine nacelles.

ENGINES

Two United Aircraft of Canada (Pratt & Whitney) PT6A–20 turboprops, each rated at 550 s.h.p. and driving a three-blade reversible-pitch airscrew. Fuel tanks in wings, with total capacity of 311 gal.

PAYLOAD

Crew of two on flight deck. Normally 14 seats in pairs with centre aisle and 15th opposite door. Baggage space in nose and behind rear seats, and provision for under-fuselage cargo and baggage pack with capacity of 800 lb. Seats are removable for all-cargo operation or for mixed cargo-passenger services with movable bulkhead between passengers and freight.

DIMENSIONS

Wing span: 45′ 10½″. *Length:* 44′ 6¾″.
Height: 14′ 4¼″. *Wing area:* 279.7 sq. ft.

WEIGHTS

Basic operating weight: 5,875 lb.
Max. take-off weight: 10,400 lb.

PERFORMANCE

Max. cruising speed: 254 m.p.h.
Service ceiling: 23,650′.
Take-off distance over 50′ obstacle: 2,222′.
Typical range: 375 miles with full payload.

Largest aircraft of Beech design currently in production, the Model 99 is widely used by local-service airlines in America and throughout the world. Deliveries began in May 1968. Little more than a year later, 91 Beechcraft 99s were in use by 32 airlines. The model 99A, also in production and service, differs in having 680 s.h.p., PT6A–27 engines and improved performance.

BERIEV Be–30 (Russia)

First Flight: **March 3, 1967**

AIRFRAME

High unswept wings, with anhedral on outer panels. Sweptback vertical tail surfaces. Conventional control surfaces and double-slotted trailing-edge flaps. Tricycle undercarriage, with single wheel on each unit. Nose-wheel retracts forward, main units rearward into engine nacelles.

ENGINES

Two Glushenkov TVD–10 turboprops, each rated at 950 h.p. Fuel tanks in wings, with total capacity of 2,205 lb.

PAYLOAD

Crew of two, or pilot and passenger on flight deck. Main cabin accommodates 14 passengers in pairs, with centre aisle. Small compartment for mail or freight forward of cabin; baggage compartment and toilet aft of cabin. All seats removable to provide clear cabin for carrying freight or, in ambulance role, nine stretcher patients, six seated casualties and an attendant.

DIMENSIONS

Wing span: 55′ 9¼″.   *Length:* 51′ 6″.
Height: 17′ 11″.   *Wing area:* 345 sq. ft.

WEIGHTS

Max. payload: 3,307 lb.
Max. take-off weight: 12,920 lb.

PERFORMANCE

Max. cruising speed: 298 m.p.h.
Take-off run: 820′.
Typical range: 807 miles at 285 m.p.h. with 1,984-lb. payload.

Under Aeroflot's massive re-equipment programme for the 'seventies, this short-haul transport is scheduled to replace the veteran An–2 biplane on all routes which do not justify use of the larger An–24 or where airfields are too small for the latter type. To get flight testing under way as quickly as possible, the prototype flew initially with 740 h.p. ASh–21 piston-engines. Production models were entering service in quantity in 1970.

BOEING 707–420 (U.S.A.)
First Flight (707 prototype): **July 15, 1954**

AIRFRAME
Low wings, swept back at 35°, with engines suspended underneath in pods. Swept tail surfaces, with small ventral fin. Lateral control by outboard and inboard ailerons and two spoilers on each wing. Variable-incidence tailplane. Conventional rudder and elevators. Small leading-edge flap between each pair of engine nacelles. Double-slotted trailing-edge flaps. Tricycle undercarriage, with twin nose-wheels and main four-wheel bogies. Main units retract inward, nose-wheels forward.

ENGINES
Four Rolls-Royce Conway Mk. 508 turbofans, each rated at 17,500 lb.s.t. Fuel tanks in wings, with total capacity of 19,863 gal.

PAYLOAD
Crew of four on flight deck. Seats for 131–189 passengers in pressurised cabin, with galleys, cloakrooms, toilets and 1,775 cu. ft. of baggage and freight space.

DIMENSIONS
Wing span: 142′ 5″. *Length:* 152′ 11″. *Height:* 42′ 5″. *Wing area:* 2,892 sq. ft.

WEIGHTS
Basic operating weight: 133,000 lb.
Max. take-off weight: 312,000 lb.

PERFORMANCE
Max. cruising speed: 593 m.p.h.
Runway length needed for take-off: 10,700′.
Typical range: 4,865 miles at 531 m.p.h. at 39,000′ with full payload.

First and most successful of the big American jet-liners, the Boeing 707 has been in airline service since 1958. By April 1970 a total of 845 had been ordered by airlines and air forces, including orders for the slightly smaller Boeing 720. There are several versions. Smallest is the 707–120 series, with 13,500 lb.s.t. Pratt & Whitney JT3C–6 engines, span of 130 ft. 10 in. and length of 144 ft. 6 in. The 707–120B is similar, but with more powerful JT3D turbofan engines. The 707–220 differs in having 15,800 lb.s.t. Pratt & Whitney JT4A–3 turbojets. The larger 707–320 Intercontinental is similar to the 707–420 described above, except that it has 16,800 lb.s.t. JT4A–9 engines. Current versions are the 707–320B, with 18,000 lb.s.t. JT3D–3B turbofans and a span of 145 ft. 9 in., and its cargo or mixed cargo/passenger counterpart, the 707–320C.

BOEING 720B (U.S.A.)

First Flight (720 prototype): **November 23, 1959**

AIRFRAME

Basically similar to that of the Boeing 707 (see page 22). Wing leading-edges extended inboard of inner engine nacelles, giving slightly increased sweepback.

ENGINES

Four Pratt & Whitney JT3D–1 turbofans, each rated at 17,000 lb.s.t. or JT3D–3s rated at 18,000 lb.s.t. Fuel tanks in wings, with total capacity of 12,410 gal.

PAYLOAD

Crew of four on flight deck. Seats for 110–167 passengers in pressurised cabin, with galleys, cloakrooms, toilets and 1,378 cu. ft. of baggage and freight space.

DIMENSIONS

Wing span: 130′ 10″. *Length:* 136′ 9″.
Height: 41′ 6½″. *Wing area:* 2,521 sq. ft.

WEIGHTS

Basic operating weight: 112,883 lb.
Max. take-off weight: 234,000 lb.

PERFORMANCE

Max. cruising speed: 611 m.p.h.
Service ceiling: 42,000′.
Take-off run: 6,400′.
Typical range: 4,155 miles at 557 m.p.h. at 40,000′ with full payload.

The Boeing 720 was a development of the Boeing 707 for use on slightly shorter routes. As less fuel is carried, it was possible to make the structure lighter. At the same time, improvements to the wing gave the 720 improved take-off performance and cruising speed.

The basic 720 is almost identical to the 707–120 in size, aerodynamic design and control systems and is powered by either 12,500 lb.s.t. Pratt & Whitney JT3C–7 or 13,000 lb.s.t. JT3C–12 turbojets. The 720B, as described above, is the turbofan version, with much improved performance. A total of 154 Boeing 720s and 720Bs were supplied to 16 airlines. As in the case of the 707, some airlines re-engined their 720s with turbofan engines to take advantage of the improved performance and operating costs.

BOEING 727-100 (U.S.A.)

First Flight: **February 9, 1963**

AIRFRAME

Low wings, swept back at 32°. Sweptback tail surfaces, with tailplane mounted at top of fin. Control surfaces on wings consist of inner and outer ailerons and spoilers, with full-span leading-edge slats and flaps, and triple-slotted trailing-edge flaps. Twin rudders and variable-incidence tailplane. Two engines in pods on sides of rear fuselage. Air intake for third engine at base of fin. Tricycle undercarriage, with twin wheels on each unit. Main units retract inward into fuselage, nose-wheels forward.

ENGINES

Three Pratt & Whitney JT8D-1 or JT8D-7 turbofans, each rated at 14,000 lb.s.t., or JT8D-9s rated at 14,500 lb.s.t. Fuel tanks in wings with max. capacity of 5,973-6,645 gal.

PAYLOAD

Crew of three on flight deck. Seats for up to 131 passengers in pressurised cabin, with two galleys, wardrobes and toilets. Underfloor holds for 900 cu. ft. of luggage.

DIMENSIONS

Wing span: 108'. *Length:* 133' 2".
Height: 34'. *Wing area:* 1,700 sq. ft.

WEIGHTS

Basic operating weight: 86,237-86,719 lb.
Max. take-off weight: 142,000-169,000 lb.

PERFORMANCE

Max. cruising speed: 605 m.p.h.
Service ceiling: 37,400'.
Take-off run: 4,980'.
Typical range: 1,900 miles with max. payload.

Boeing produced their competitor to Britain's Trident by utilising much of the fuselage and many of the systems of the already-proven Boeing 720. This helped them to get the 727 into service before the Trident, after starting work more than 18 months later.

In addition to the basic 727-100 (described and illustrated), there is the 727-200 with 20-ft. longer fuselage, seating up to 189 passengers, and optional 15,000 lb.s.t. JT8D-11 engines; and the 727-100C and 727-100QC convertible cargo-passenger versions of the ' 100 '.

By April 1970, a total of 827 Boeing 727s had been sold and 786 delivered. Overseas customers include Lufthansa, Trans-Australia Airlines and Ansett-ANA.

BOEING 737–200 (U.S.A.)
First Flight (737 Prototype): **April 9, 1967**

AIRFRAME
Low wings, swept back at 25°, with engines suspended beneath in pods. Swept tail surfaces. Lateral control by aileron and two-section flight spoilers on each wing. Variable-incidence tailplane. Conventional rudder and elevators. Krueger flap inboard of nacelle and three-section slat outboard of nacelle on each wing leading-edge. Triple-slotted trailing-edge flaps. Flight spoilers operate as air-brakes in flight. Two further ground spoilers on each wing are used during landing. Tricycle undercarriage, with twin-wheels on each unit. Nose-wheels retract forward, main units inward.

ENGINES
Two Pratt & Whitney JT8D–9 turbofans, each rated at 14,500 lb.s.t. or JT8D–7s rated at 14,000 lb.s.t. Fuel tanks in wings and centre-section, with total capacity of 2,382–3,983 gal.

PAYLOAD
Crew of two on flight deck. Seats in pressurised cabin for up to 115–125 passengers, with galleys, toilets and 875 cu. ft. of underfloor baggage and cargo space.

DIMENSIONS
Wing span: 93'.
Height: 37'
Length: 100'.
Wing area: 980 sq. ft.

WEIGHTS
Basic operating weight: 58,607–59,651 lb.
Max. take-off weight: 109,000–114,500 lb.

PERFORMANCE (JT8D–9 engines)
Max. speed: 586 m.p.h.
Take-off distance over 35' obstacle: 7,100' (at 109,000 lb. weight).
Typical range: 2,135 miles with 115 passengers.

Smallest member of the Boeing jet transport family, the short-range Model 737 has the same fuselage cross-section as its bigger brothers and uses many components of the 727. It also has the same JT8D engines, but reverts to underwing pods. The original 737–100 series, with shorter fuselage and, usually, JT8D–7 engines, carries 103–115 passengers. There are also convertible passenger-freight (200C), quick-change passenger-freight (200QC) and business jet versions of the Model 737–200. A total of 260 Model 737s had been sold and 236 delivered by April 1, 1970.

BOEING 747 (U.S.A.)

First Flight: **February 9, 1969**

AIRFRAME

Low wings swept back at 37° 30′ with engines suspended underneath in pods. Swept tail surfaces. Lateral control by low-speed outboard ailerons, high-speed inboard ailerons and four flight spoilers on each wing. Variable-incidence tailplane. Conventional two-section rudder and elevators. Three-section Krueger flap inboard and ten-section leading-edge flap outboard on each wing. Triple-slotted trailing-edge flaps. Two-section ground spoiler above each wing. Tricycle under-carriage, with forward-retracting twin nose-wheel unit and four four-wheel bogie main units, two retracting forward into fuselage and two inward into wing roots.

ENGINES

Four Pratt & Whitney JT9D–3 turbofans, each rated at 43,500 lb.s.t. Fuel tanks in wings, with total capacity of 39,310 gal.

PAYLOAD

Crew of three on flight deck, with seats for two observers. Max. accommodation for 490 passengers in ten-abreast seating, with two aisles. Freight and baggage holds with capacity of 6,250 cu. ft. under cabin floor. Lounge or private cabins on upper deck aft of flight deck. Galleys on lower deck, with lifts to main cabin level.

DIMENSIONS

Wing span: 195′ 8″.   *Length:* 231′ 4″.
Height: 63′ 5″.   *Wing area:* 5,500 sq. ft.

WEIGHTS

Basic operating weight: 348,816 lb.
Max. take-off weight: 710,000 lb.

PERFORMANCE

Max. speed: 595 m.p.h.
Cruise ceiling: 45,000′.
Take-off distance to 35′: 10,400′.
Typical range: 5,790 miles with 374 passengers.

Largest airliner yet in service, the 747 justifies its nickname of ' Jumbo-jet '. It entered service with Pan American in January 1970, each aircraft being equipped initially with 362 seats, replacing two Boeing 707s and offering such comfort that Pan Am trans-atlantic traffic increased by 106% within three months. Orders totalled 191 by April 1, 1970, including later passenger (747B), convertible (747C) and all-cargo (747F) versions with weight increased to 775,000 lb.

BOEING-VERTOL 107 Model II (U.S.A.)

First Flight: **April 22, 1958**

AIRFRAME

Typical tandem-rotor helicopter layout, with both rotors mounted atop pylons above fuselage. Engines buried in base of rear pylon. Non-retractable tricycle undercarriage, with twin wheels on each unit. Fuselage is sealed, to permit operation from water. Sponsons at rear act as stabilising floats on water.

ENGINES

Two General Electric CT58–110 shaft-turbines, each rated at 1,250 h.p. Fuel tanks in sponsons.

PAYLOAD

Crew of two on flight deck. Seats for 25 passengers, three-abreast, in cabin. Roll-out baggage container in underside of rear fuselage.

DIMENSIONS

Rotor diameter: each 50′. *Length:* 44′ 7″.
Height: 16′ 10″.

WEIGHTS

Empty: 10,732 lb.
Max. take-off weight: 19,000 lb.

PERFORMANCE

Max. speed: 168 m.p.h.
Service ceiling: 13,000′.
Typical range: 109 miles at 150 m.p.h. at 5,000′ with 6,600-lb. payload.

One of the neatest airline helicopters yet built, the Boeing-Vertol 107 is in service with New York Airways, who acquired seven for their network of services in the New York area. Military versions for the U.S. Marine Corps and Navy, designated CH–46 and UH–46 respectively, have a rear loading ramp for quick loading and unloading in combat areas. Boeing continue to be responsible for military versions, which are in service in several countries, but all production of commercial 107s is undertaken under licence by Kawasaki of Japan. Latest Kawasaki version is the KV–107/IIA with 1,500 h.p. CT58–140–1 engines.

BRISTOL 170 Mk. 32 FREIGHTER (Great Britain)

First Flight (170 prototype): **December 2, 1945**

AIRFRAME

High unswept wings. Unswept tail surfaces, with large dorsal fin. Conventional control surfaces and split trailing-edge flaps. Non-retractable tail-wheel undercarriage.

ENGINES

Two Bristol Hercules 734 fourteen-cylinder two-row radial engines, each rated at 2,000 h.p. and driving a four-blade airscrew. Fuel tanks in wings, with total capacity of 1,170 gal.

PAYLOAD

Crew of two or three on flight deck. Normal load consists of up to three motor-cars in main hold, plus 12–20 passengers in small cabin at rear. Can be equipped with 60 passenger seats.

DIMENSIONS

Wing span: 108'.　　　*Length:* 73' 6".
Height: 21' 8".　　*Wing area:* 1,487 sq. ft.

WEIGHTS

Empty: 29,465 lb.
Max. take-off weight: 44,000 lb.

PERFORMANCE

Max. speed: 195 m.p.h.
Service ceiling: 24,500'.
Typical range: 490 miles at 166 m.p.h. at 5,000' with full payload.

As the war against Japan drew to a close, the Air Ministry was planning to order for the R.A.F. a sturdy, simple transport aircraft that would be able to operate into and out of jungle airstrips. Bristol decided to continue the project after the war and adapted it into the Type 170 Freighter for commercial use. Beauty took second place to efficiency. The crew were put above the main cabin, and large nose loading doors were fitted. This meant that heavy freight and vehicles could be loaded straight from lorries or up a short ramp into the hold.

Altogether 214 Freighters were built. They made possible the cross-Channel vehicle ferry services pioneered by Silver City Airways in 1948, and eventually the special ' long-nose ' Mk. 32 version, described above, was evolved to provide room for three cars instead of two. Eight of these remained in service with British Air Ferries until 1970.

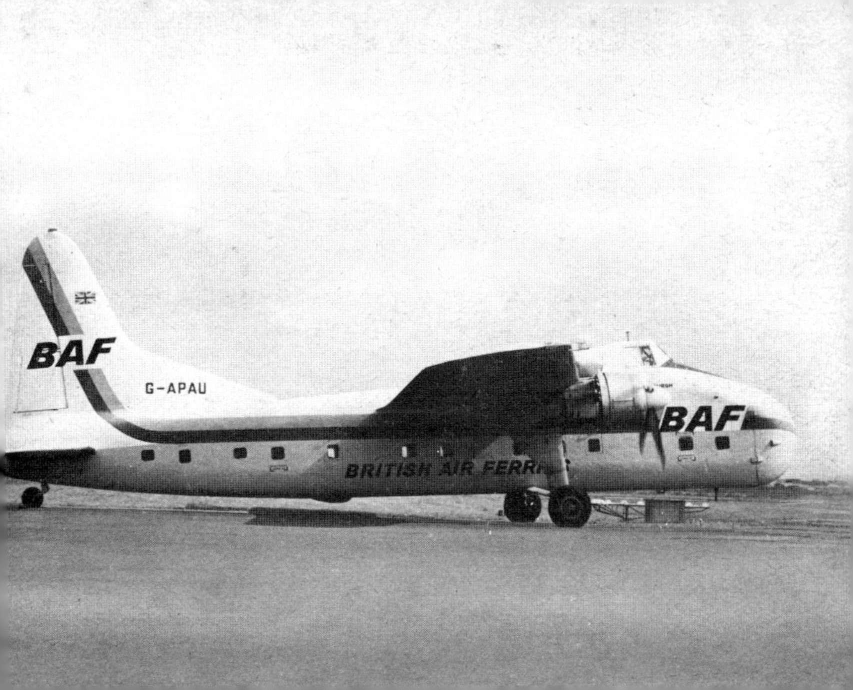
BAF
G-APAU
BAF
BRITISH AIR FERR

BRISTOL 175 BRITANNIA 312 (Great Britain)

First Flight: **August 16, 1952**

AIRFRAME

Low unswept wings. Unswept tail surfaces. Conventional control surfaces and double-slotted trailing-edge flaps. Tricycle undercarriage, with twin nose-wheels and four-wheel bogie main units. Nose-wheels retract forward, main units backward into rear of inner engine nacelles.

ENGINES

Four Bristol Siddeley Proteus 765 turbo-props, each rated at 4,445 h.p. and driving a four-blade reversible-pitch airscrew. Fuel tanks in wings, with total capacity of 8,580 gal.

PAYLOAD

Flight and cabin crew of nine, and up to 133 passengers in pressurised cabin.

DIMENSIONS

Wing span: 142′ 3½″.　*Length:* 124′ 3″.
Height: 37′ 6″.　*Wing area:* 2,075 sq. ft.

WEIGHTS

Empty: 93,100 lb.
Max. take-off weight: 185,000 lb.

PERFORMANCE

Max. cruising speed: 405 m.p.h.
Typical range: 4,270 miles at 355 m.p.h. at 25,000′ with full payload.

It was intended originally to order for B.O.A.C. a version of the Britannia with a span of 130 ft., four Centaurus piston-engines and seats for 42 passengers. Instead, the prototypes were built with a span of 140 ft., four of the new Proteus turboprops and room for 64 passengers. B.O.A.C. decided to order 15, and the first of these entered service in 1957, under the designation Britannia 102, with 3,890 h.p. Proteus 705 engines. The 114-ft. long fuselage of the Britannia 102 accommodated up to 92 passengers. In the second version ordered by B.O.A.C., the Britannia 312, the fuselage was lengthened by just over 10 ft. and this became standard on subsequent versions. At the same time, more powerful engines were introduced. Altogether, 82 Britannias were sold to airlines and the R.A.F.; most of the commercial models remain in service with British independent airlines and foreign operators.

BRITTEN-NORMAN BN–2A ISLANDER (Great Britain)

First Flight: **June 13, 1965**

AIRFRAME

High unswept wings with distinctive turned-up tips. Unswept tail surfaces. Conventional control surfaces, with slotted ailerons and slotted trailing-edge flaps. Non-retractable tricycle undercarriage, with single nose-wheel and twin wheels on each main unit. Cantilever main legs under engine nacelles. Square-section fuselage.

ENGINES

Two Lycoming O–540–E4C5 six-cylinder horizontally-opposed air-cooled engines, each rated at 260 h.p. and driving a Hartzell two-blade airscrew. Two fuel tanks in wings, capacity 111 gal.

PAYLOAD

Up to ten persons in pairs, with baggage space at rear. Cabin can also be arranged for executive, ambulance, freight or parachuting use.

DIMENSIONS

Wing span: 49′. *Length:* 35′ 8″.
Height: 13′ 8″. *Wing area:* 325 sq. ft.

WEIGHTS

Basic operating weight: 4,122 lb.
Max. take-off weight: 6,300 lb.

PERFORMANCE

Max. cruising speed: 160 m.p.h.
Service ceiling: 14,600′.
Take-off run: 560′.
Typical range: 425 miles at 153 m.p.h. at 13,000′ with max. payload.

This inexpensive and highly practical little aircraft has been developed as a replacement for types like the Dragon Rapide biplane. The prototype was developed as a private venture and flew only 14 months after design work began. It was powered originally by 210 h.p. Continental engines and spanned 45 ft., but production Islanders are more powerful, with a longer span, as described and illustrated. British Hovercraft Corporation had to be called in to cope with production of more than three aircraft a week by 1969. An Islander won the BP England-Australia Air Race in December of that year. New versions, with supercharged and more powerful engines are under development.

CANADAIR FORTY-FOUR (Canada)

First Flight: **November 16, 1960**

AIRFRAME

Basically similar to that of Bristol Britannia, but with considerable structural redesign to take more powerful engines and permit higher loaded weight. Entire tail unit is hinged to swing round to starboard for quick loading of freight.

ENGINES

Four Rolls-Royce Tyne R.Ty.12 turbo-props, each rated at 5,730 h.p. and driving a four-blade reversible-pitch airscrew. Fuel tanks in wings and centre-section, with total capacity of 10,150 gal.

PAYLOAD

Intended mainly for use as a freighter. Cabin has capacity of 6,380 cu. ft. and, together with the under-floor freight hold, can carry up to 64,372 lb. of cargo. A mixed passenger-freight version can carry 124 passengers and 1,700 cu. ft. of cargo.

DIMENSIONS

Wing span: 142′ 3½″. *Length:* 136′ 10″. *Height:* 38′ 8″. *Wing area:* 2,075 sq. ft.

WEIGHTS

Basic operating weight: 88,952 lb.
Max. take-off weight: 210,000 lb.

PERFORMANCE

Max. cruising speed: 402 m.p.h.
Take-off run: 6,800′.
Typical range: 5,660 miles at 386 m.p.h. at 20,000′ with 37,300-lb. payload.

Although derived from the Britannia, the Canadair Forty-Four was extensively redesigned for its role as a specialised freighter and has Tyne engines of far greater power than the Proteus turboprops fitted in the original version.

Twelve CL-44s, with conventional side-loading doors, were ordered for the R.C.A.F. and are in service under the designation CC-106 Yukon. They were followed by the commercial Forty-Four, with a swing-tail to permit 'straight-in' loading into the rear of the cabin. By the spring of 1967, Forty-Fours were being operated mainly by Airlift International, Tradewinds, Trans-Mediterranean and Trans-Meridian. The Loftleidir (Icelandic) aircraft have a 15-ft. longer fuselage, accommodating up to 214 passengers, and are designated CL-44J or Canadair 400.

CONVAIR 640 (U.S.A.)

First Flight (Convair 240 prototype): **March 16, 1947**

AIRFRAME
Low unswept wings. Unswept tail surfaces. Conventional control surfaces and trailing-edge flaps. Tricycle undercarriage, with twin wheels on each unit. All units retract forward.

ENGINES
Two Rolls-Royce Dart R.Da.10 Mk. 542–4 turboprops, each rated at 3,025 h.p. and driving a four-blade reversible-pitch airscrew. Fuel tanks in wings, with total capacity of 1,440 or 2,452 gal.

PAYLOAD
Crew of three or four, and 44–56 passengers in pressurised cabin. Baggage and freight holds fore and aft of cabin and under floor.

DIMENSIONS
Wing span: 105′ 4″.   *Length:* 81′ 6″.
Height: 28′ 2″.   *Wing area:* 963.8 sq. ft.

WEIGHTS
Basic operating weight: 30,275 lb.
Max. take-off weight: 55,000 lb.

PERFORMANCE
Max. speed: 300 m.p.h.

Service ceiling: 23,000′.
Typical range: 1,230 miles at 300 m.p.h. at 15,000′ with standard fuel.

Since the war, companies all over the world have tried to produce a replacement for the veteran DC–3. The Convair 240, which flew in 1947, came into this category, with a span of 91 ft. 9 in. and seats for 40 passengers. A total of 176 were built, before the 240 was superseded by the Convair 340. This flew for the first time on October 5, 1951, and introduced larger-span wings, a longer fuselage accommodating 44 passengers and other changes. When 209 Convair 340s had been produced they were followed in turn by the Convair 440 Metropolitan, with redesigned engine nacelles and other improvements to reduce noise inside the cabin and increase performance; 186 were built. Many Convairs have been re-engined with Allison 501 (Convair 580) or Rolls-Royce Dart (Convair 600/640) turboprops, as described and illustrated, mainly for service in North America. Transport and training versions of the Convair 240, 340 and 440 are in service with the U.S. armed forces.

CONVAIR 880-M (U.S.A.)

First Flight: **January 27, 1959**

AIRFRAME

Low wings, swept back at 35°, with engines suspended underneath in pods. Swept tail surfaces. Lateral control by linked ailerons and spoilers. Variable-incidence tailplane. Conventional rudder and elevators. Leading-edge slats. Double-slotted trailing-edge flaps. Tricycle undercarriage, with twin nose-wheels and main four-wheel bogies. Main units retract inward, nose-wheels forward.

ENGINES

Four General Electric CJ805–3B turbojets, each rated at 11,650 lb.s.t. Fuel tanks in wings and centre-section, with max. capacity of 10,437 gal.

PAYLOAD

Crew of five, and seats for 88–110 passengers in pressurised cabin, with up to four galleys, two toilets and optional 12-seat club lounge. Two cargo holds with total volume of 849 cu. ft.

DIMENSIONS

Wing span: 120′. *Length:* 129′ 4″.
Height: 36′ 4″. *Wing area:* 2,000 sq. ft.

WEIGHTS

Basic operating weight: 94,000 lb.
Max. take-off weight: 193,000 lb.

PERFORMANCE

Max. cruising speed: 615 m.p.h.
Take-off run: 7,550′.
Typical range: 2,880 miles at 541 m.p.h. at 35,000′ with full payload.

Announced in 1956, the Convair 880 was intended as a medium-size, high-speed jetliner for use on medium-length routes. Forty-eight of the basic model 880s were delivered to T.W.A., Northeast Airlines and Delta Air Lines, each powered by four 11,200 lb.s.t. CJ805–3 turbojets. The 13 model 880-Ms still operated by Japan Air Lines and Cathay Pacific Airways have more powerful engines, four leading-edge slats and other changes to improve take-off performance from short runways.

CONVAIR 990A CORONADO (U.S.A.)

First Flight: **January 24, 1961**

AIRFRAME

Basically similar to that of Convair 880, but with longer fuselage, redesigned wing trailing-edge and two tapered fairings to reduce drag on trailing-edge of each wing.

ENGINES

Four General Electric CJ805–23B turbo-fans, each rated at 16,050 lb.s.t. Fuel tanks in wings, centre-section and trailing-edge fairings, with capacity of 12,589 gal. in basic 990 and 12,958 gal. in over-water 990 Coronado.

PAYLOAD

Crew of five, and seats for up to 106 passengers in ·pressurised cabin. Two baggage and freight holds with combined volume of 928 cu. ft.

DIMENSIONS

Wing span: 120′. *Length:* 139′ 5″.
Height: 39′ 6″. *Wing area:* 2,250 sq. ft.

WEIGHTS

Basic operating weight: 120,900 lb.
Max. take-off weight: 253,000 lb.

PERFORMANCE

Max. cruising speed: 625 m.p.h.
Take-off run: 9,800′.
Typical range: 3,920 miles at 537 m.p.h. at 35,000′ with max. payload.

The Convair 990A was developed from the 880 to take advantage of the increased power and better economy of the CJ805–23B turbo-fan engine, and is one of the world's fastest production jet-liners, with a maximum cruising speed of 625 m.p.h. Thirty-six were delivered to Aerolineas Peruanas, Garuda Indonesian Airways, Swissair, Balair, VARIG of Brazil. M. E. A., Modern Air Transport, Spantax and Alaska Airlines.

DE HAVILLAND DHC-3 OTTER (Canada)

First Flight: **December 12, 1951**

AIRFRAME

High unswept wings, with single bracing strut each side. Unswept tail surfaces. Conventional control surfaces and double-slotted flaps. Non-retractable tail-wheel undercarriage, with single wheel on each unit. Can be fitted with floats, skis or combined wheel-and-float amphibious gear.

ENGINE

One Pratt & Whitney R–1340 nine-cylinder radial engine, rated at 600 h.p. and driving a three-blade airscrew. Fuel tanks under cabin floor, with capacity of 178 gal.

PAYLOAD

Crew of two or pilot and passenger on flight deck. Seats for up to 10 passengers in cabin, or fittings for up to six stretchers and four seats. With seats removed there is 345 cu. ft. of cargo space.

DIMENSIONS

Wing span: 58'.
Height: 12' 7".
Length: 41' 10".
Wing area: 375 sq. ft.

WEIGHTS

Empty: 4,431 lb.
Max. take-off weight: 8,000 lb.

PERFORMANCE

Max. speed: 160 m.p.h.
Service ceiling: 18,800'.
Max. range: 945 miles at 138 m.p.h. at 5,000'.

More than 450 of these extremely useful single-engined STOL transports were built. Of these, 269 were delivered to the U.S. Army and Navy; but others are used throughout the world for commercial purposes, their short landing and take-off runs making them ideal in places where airfields are few and far between. The fact that the wheels can be replaced by floats or skis in winter enables the Otter to provide year-round service in regions like the far north of Canada, and it is no coincidence that ten nations have used Otters and smaller DHC-2 Beavers for duty in the Antarctic.

DE HAVILLAND DHC-4 CARIBOU (Canada)

First Flight: **July 30, 1958**

AIRFRAME

High unswept wings, with anhedral on centre-section, giving a ' cranked ' appearance in front view. Unswept tail surfaces, with tailplane mounted part-way up fin. Full-span double-slotted flaps, outer portions acting as ailerons. Conventional rudder and elevators. Rear fuselage sharply upswept, with loading ramp for vehicles in undersurface. Tricycle undercarriage, with twin wheels on each unit. Nose-wheels retract rearward, main units forward into engine nacelles.

ENGINES

Two Pratt & Whitney R-2000-7M2 fourteen-cylinder two-row radial engines, each rated at 1,450 h.p. and driving a three-blade airscrew. Fuel tanks in wings, with total capacity of 690 gal.

PAYLOAD

Crew of two on flight deck. Seats for 30 passengers in main cabin, or alternative freight load.

DIMENSIONS

Wing span: 95' 7½". *Length:* 72' 7".
Height: 31' 9". *Wing area:* 912 sq. ft.

WEIGHTS

Empty: 17,485 lb.
Max. take-off weight: 28,500 lb.

PERFORMANCE

Max. speed: 216 m.p.h.
Service ceiling: 24,800'.
Take-off run: 725'.
Typical range: 240 miles at 182 m.p.h. at 7,500' with 8,740-lb. payload.

After many years' experience with their Beaver and Otter STOL (short take-off and landing) aircraft, de Havilland of Canada decided in 1956 to build a twin-engined STOL transport: the result was the Caribou, which combines STOL performance with the load-carrying ability of the DC-3.

Most of the 286 Caribous delivered so far are used on military duties, including large numbers for the U.S. Air Force under the designation C-7A. These carry 32 troops, 26 fully equipped paratroops, or 22 stretcher patients, four sitting casualties and four attendants. Freight loads include three tons of cargo or two fully loaded Jeeps. Airline users include Air Asia of Taiwan and Ansett-MAL in New Guinea.

DE HAVILLAND DHC–6 TWIN OTTER Srs.200 (Canada)

First Flight (Srs.100 Prototype): **May 20, 1965**

AIRFRAME
High unswept wings, with single bracing strut each side. Swept vertical tail surfaces. Conventional control surfaces and double-slotted flaps. Ailerons droop with flaps. Non-retractable tricycle undercarriage, with single wheel on each unit. Can be fitted with floats or wheel-skis.

ENGINES
Two United Aircraft of Canada (Pratt & Whitney) PT6A–20 turboprops, each rated at 579 h.p. and driving a three-blade reversible-pitch airscrew. Fuel tanks under cabin floor, with total capacity of 315 gal.

PAYLOAD
One or two pilots side-by-side on flight deck. Up to 19 passengers in main cabin, with space for 800 lb. of baggage and freight in compartments in nose and aft of cabin. Can be equipped for cargo, survey, ambulance or executive duties.

DIMENSIONS
Wing span: 65'.   *Length:* 51' 9".   *Height:* 18' 7".   *Wing area:* 420 sq. ft.

WEIGHTS
Basic operating weight: 6,515 lb.
Max. take-off weight: 11,579 lb.

PERFORMANCE
Max. cruising speed: 190 m.p.h.
Service ceiling: 24,300'.
Take-off distance to 50': 1,230–1,900'.
Typical range: 945 miles with max. fuel.

As its name implies, the Twin Otter was conceived as a twin-turboprop development of the Otter, using many components of the latter. The original Srs.100 version differs from the 200 (described and illustrated) mainly in having a shorter nose and smaller baggage compartments. The latest Srs.300 has 652 h.p. PT6A–27 engines; the first to be delivered in the spring of 1969 was the 231st Twin Otter built by D.H. Canada. Many are used by local service airlines, their short take-off and landing capabilities enabling them to operate from very short airstrips.

DORNIER Do 28D–1 SKYSERVANT (Germany)

First Flight (Do 28D Prototype): **February 23, 1966**

AIRFRAME

High unswept wings. Unswept angular tail surfaces, with large fin and rudder. Conventional ailerons, double-slotted trailing-edge flaps and all-moving horizontal tail surfaces. Engines and main undercarriage carried at tips of short stub-wings. Non-retractable tail-wheel undercarriage, with optional spats on main wheels.

ENGINES

Two Lycoming IGSO–540 six-cylinder horizontally-opposed air-cooled engines, each rated at 380 h.p. and driving a three-blade airscrew. Fuel tanks in engine nacelles, with total capacity of 181 gal.

PAYLOAD

Crew of two or pilot and passenger on flight deck. Main cabin accommodates 12 seats in pairs with centre aisle, or 13 inward-facing seats, or five stretchers and five seats. Toilet and/or baggage compartment aft of cabin. Further baggage space in nose. Seats removable to clear cabin for freight carrying.

DIMENSIONS

Wing span: 50′ 10¼″.　*Length:* 38′ 0¾″.
Height: 12′ 10″.　*Wing area:* 308 sq. ft.

WEIGHTS

Basic operating weight: 4,775 lb.
Max. take-off weight: 8,050 lb.

PERFORMANCE

Max. speed: 199 m.p.h.
Service ceiling: 24,300′.
Take-off distance to 50′: 1,140–1,700′.
Typical range: 1,125 miles at 143 m.p.h. with max. fuel.

Despite its designation, this light transport is an entirely new design, bearing only a superficial resemblance to the smaller Do 28. The original Do 28D Skyservant had a span of only 49′ 2½″ and was built in small numbers before being superseded by the current Do 28D–1, as described and illustrated. Orders, including 121 for the German armed forces, are being filled at the rate of five aircraft per month. Many have been exported to the U.S.A.

DOUGLAS DC–3 DAKOTA (U.S.A.)

First Flight: **December 22, 1935**

AIRFRAME

Low wings with sweptback leading-edges. Conventional control surfaces and trailing-edge flaps. Tail-wheel undercarriage, with single wheel on each unit. Main wheels retract partially into engine nacelles.

ENGINES

Two Pratt & Whitney R–1830 fourteen-cylinder two-row radial engines, each rated at 1,200 h.p. and driving a three-blade airscrew. Fuel tanks in wings with total capacity of 680 gal.

PAYLOAD

Crew of three on flight deck. Seats for up to 36 passengers in main cabin, with buffet, toilet and baggage compartments.

DIMENSIONS

Wing span: 95′. *Length:* 64′ 5″.
Height: 16′ 11″. *Wing area:* 987 sq. ft.

WEIGHTS

Basic operating weight: 16,600 lb.
Max. take-off weight: 28,000 lb.

PERFORMANCE

Max. speed: 216 m.p.h.
Service ceiling: 23,200′
Typical range: 1,100 miles at 178 m.p.h. at 5,000′.

No other airliner in the world has played such an important role in the development of air transport as the DC-3. Although it has now been in service for over 35 years, it still outnumbers most other types of aircraft in airline use and is likely to continue for many more years as a local-service and charter airliner.

The DC-3 began life in two forms, as the 14-passenger Douglas D.S.T. (Douglas sleeper transport) and 21-passenger DC-3. It had already made a name for itself when World War II started and it was adopted as the standard Allied medium-range military transport. Many of the 10,123 built during the war, under military designations such as C-47 and C-53, were converted later for civil use and 803 new DC-3s were also built after the war.

DOUGLAS DC–4 SKYMASTER (U.S.A.)

First Flight: **June 7, 1938**

AIRFRAME

Low unswept wings. Unswept tail unit. Conventional control surfaces and slotted flaps. Tricycle undercarriage, with single nose-wheel and twin-wheel main units. All units retract forward, the main wheels into the inner engine nacelles.

ENGINES

Four Pratt & Whitney R–2000 fourteen-cylinder two-row radial engines, each rated at 1,450 h.p. and driving a three-blade airscrew. Fuel tanks in wings, with capacity of 3,000 gal.

PAYLOAD

Crew of five. Seats for up to 86 passengers in cabin, with galley, toilets, cloakroom and baggage compartments.

DIMENSIONS

Wing span: 117′ 6″.   *Length:* 93′ 11″.
Height: 27′ 6½″.   *Wing area:* 1,462 sq. ft.

WEIGHTS

Empty: 40,806 lb.
Max. take-off weight: 73,800 lb.

PERFORMANCE

Max. speed: 280 m.p.h.
Service ceiling: 22,500′.
Typical range: 2,140 miles at 201 m.p.h. at 10,000′ with max. payload.

The DC-3 was such a world-beater that U.S. airlines soon began asking Douglas for a bigger, four-engined airliner of equally advanced design. So, in 1938, Douglas produced the prototype DC-4. Its general layout and construction followed closely those of the DC-3, but it was powered by four 1,450 h.p. Pratt & Whitney Twin-Hornet engines, had three fins and rudders and introduced a tricycle undercarriage. It was fitted with 42 seats, but there was clearly room for more, and a modified version was put into production with R-2000 Twin-Wasp engines, single fin and rudder and 52 seats. Before it could be delivered, America was at war and the DC-4s were taken over by the U.S.A.A.F. and put into military service with the designation C-54. Eventually, 1,084 military C-54s were built, followed by 79 commercial DC-4s. Many of the military aircraft were converted for airline use and are still serving throughout the world side-by-side with the civil version.

DOUGLAS DC-6 and DC-7 SERIES (U.S.A.)

First Flight (DC-6): February 15, 1946

AIRFRAME
Basically similar to that of the DC-4, but larger, as described below.

ENGINES
(DC-7C). Four Wright R-3350-18EA4 Turbo Compound eighteen-cylinder two-row radial engines, each rated at 3,400 h.p. and driving a four-blade reversible-pitch airscrew. Fuel tanks in wings, with capacity of 6,515 gal.

PAYLOAD
Crew of three to five on flight deck. Seats for 54-108 passengers in DC-6B, 69-105 in DC-7C, in pressurised cabin, with galley, toilets, cloakroom and baggage compartments.

DIMENSIONS
(DC-7C). *Wing span:* 127' 6". *Length:* 112' 3".
Height: 31' 8". *Wing area:* 1,637 sq. ft.

WEIGHTS
(DC-7C). *Empty:* 72,512 lb.
Max. take-off weight: 143,000 lb.

PERFORMANCE
Max. speed: 398 m.p.h.
Service ceiling: 21,700'.
Runway length required for take-off: 6,360'.
Max. range: 5,635 miles at 274 m.p.h. at 15,000' with 15,310-lb. payload.

There is no better example of how a good aeroplane can be developed into a whole series of even-better aeroplanes than the DC-4/DC-6/DC-7 family. The DC-6 was evolved soon after the war as a larger, more powerful and pressurised successor to the DC-4, with 48-58 seats, 2,400 h.p. Pratt & Whitney R-2800 CA-15 engines and a length of 100 ft. 7 in. The DC-6A passenger/freighter was similar, except for an increase in length to 105 ft. 7 in. The DC-6B came next, as a purely passenger-carrying counterpart of the DC-6A with either 2,400 h.p. R-2800 CB-16 or 2,500 h.p. R-2800 CB-17 engines. A switch to 3,250 h.p. Turbo Compound engines was made in the DC-7, which was 108 ft. 11 in. long, and the longer-range DC-7B. Finally came the very-long-range DC-7C Seven Seas, with increased span, as described above. A total of 1,041 aircraft of the DC-6/DC-7 series were built and many examples of each remain in service. Some DC-7s were converted into DC-7F Speed-freighter specialised cargo carriers.

DOUGLAS DC-8 SUPER 63 (U.S.A.)

First Flight (DC-8 Series 10): **May 30, 1958**

AIRFRAME

Low wings, swept back at 30°, with four engines suspended in pods underneath. Sweptback tail surfaces. Variable-incidence tailplane. Conventional ailerons, elevators and rudder. Double-slotted trailing-edge flaps. Fixed leading-edge slots inboard of each engine pylon. Tricycle undercarriage, with twin-wheel nose unit and four-wheel bogies on main units. Nose-wheels retract forward, main units inward.

ENGINES

Four Pratt & Whitney JT3D-7 turbofans, each rated at 19,000 lb.s.t. Fuel tanks in wings, with max. capacity of 20,213 gal.

PAYLOAD

Crew of three to five on flight deck. Seats for up to 259 passengers in pressurised cabin. Freight and baggage compartments under floor with capacity of 2,500 cu. ft.

DIMENSIONS

Wing span: 148′ 5″.   *Length:* 187′ 5″.
Height: 42′ 5″.   *Wing area:* 2,927 sq. ft.

WEIGHTS

Empty: 153,749 lb.
Max. take-off weight: 350,000 lb.

PERFORMANCE

Max. cruising speed: 600 m.p.h.
Take-off run: 11,500′.
Max. range: 4,500 miles with max. payload.

The original versions of the DC-8 (Series 10 to 50) all have the same basic airframe, with span of 142 ft. 5 in. and length of 150 ft. 6 in. The Series 10, intended for domestic services, has 13,500 lb.s.t. Pratt & Whitney JT3C-6 turbojets and loaded weight of only 273,000 lb. The Series 20 is similar, but has 15,800 lb. JT4A-3 engines. First of the intercontinental versions, with extra fuel, was the DC-8 Series 30, with 16,800 lb.s.t. JT4A-9 or 17,500 lb. JT4A-11 turbojets. The Series 40 and 50 are similar to the 30, but have Conway and JT3D turbofan engines respectively.

First of the 'stretched' Super 60 Series, with JT3D-3B turbofans, was the Super 61, with 36 ft. 11 in. longer fuselage, seating 259 passengers. The Super 62 is only 157 ft. 5 in. long but has 6-ft. greater span and more fuel. The Super 63 (described and illustrated) combines the long fuselage of the 61 with the long-span wings of the 62.

Total orders for all DC-8s, including passenger/freight and all-freighter models, were 547 by early 1970.

DOUGLAS DC-9 SERIES 10 (U.S.A.)

First Flight: **February 25, 1965**

AIRFRAME
Low wings, swept back at 24°. Swept-back tail surfaces, with variable-incidence tailplane mounted at tip of fin. Each wing fitted with two-section aileron, three-section speed-brake and double-slotted flaps. Conventional rudder and elevator. Engines mounted on each side of rear fuselage. Tricycle undercarriage, with twin wheels on each unit. Nose-wheels retract forward, main wheels inward.

ENGINES
Two Pratt & Whitney JT8D-5 turbofans, each rated at 12,250 lb.s.t. or JT8D-1 turbofans each rated at 14,000 lb.s.t. Fuel tanks in wings, with total capacity of 2,320 gal. or 3,080 gal. respectively.

PAYLOAD
Crew of two on flight deck. Seats in pressurised cabin for up to 90 passengers with toilets at rear and provision for galley. Two underfloor baggage holds with capacity of 600 cu. ft.

DIMENSIONS
Wing span: 89′ 5″.   Length: 104′ 5″.
Height: 27′ 6″.   Wing area: 934 sq. ft.

WEIGHTS
Basic operating weight: 45,300–47,750 lb.
Max. take-off weight: 77,700–90,700 lb.

PERFORMANCE
Max. cruising speed: 561 m.p.h. at 25,000′.
Take-off run: 5,300′.
Max. range: 1,311 miles with 50 passengers.

Smallest in the current DC series of Douglas commercial transports, the DC-9 is America's counterpart to the BAC One-Eleven. In addition to the basic Series 10 version described above and illustrated, a long-range model is available, with increased fuel load, raising the take-off weight to 90,700 lb. The DC-9 Series 20 has an increased span of 93 ft. 5 in. and 14,500 lb.s.t. JT8D-9 engines. The series 30 combines the long-span wings with 14,000 lb.s.t. JT8D-7 engines and a 15-ft. longer fuselage, seating up to 115 passengers. The Series 40 differs from the 30 in having JT8D-9s and extra fuel. The Series 30 and 40 also have full-span leading-edge slats and double-slotted flaps. A total of 628 DC-9s had been ordered by early 1970, when 550 had been delivered.

FOKKER F.27 FRIENDSHIP Mk. 200 (Netherlands)

First Flight (Prototype): **November 24, 1955**

AIRFRAME

High unswept wings. Unswept tail surfaces, with dihedral on tailplane. Conventional control surfaces and slotted flaps. Tricycle undercarriage with single nose-wheel and twin-wheel main units. Nose-wheel retracts forward, main units backward into engine nacelles.

ENGINES

Two Rolls-Royce Dart Mk. 514–7 turbo-props, each rated at 1,715 h.p. in Mk. 100 and 300 aircraft. Two Rolls-Royce Dart Mk. 532–7, each rated at 2,255 h.p., in Mk. 200, 400, 500 and 600. Four-blade reversible-pitch airscrews. Fuel tanks in wings, with capacity of 1,130 gal., can be supplemented by two 200-gal. underwing tanks.

PAYLOAD

Crew of two or three on flight deck. Seats for 40–52 passengers in pressurised cabin of Mk. 200 and 600, and 52–56 in Mk. 500, with pantry and toilet. Up to 269 cu. ft. freight capacity, depending on seating.

DIMENSIONS

Wing span: 95′ 2″.
Length: 77′ 3½″ (Series 500 82′ 2½″).

Height: 27′ 11″.   *Wing area:* 754 sq. ft.

WEIGHTS

(Mk. 200).   *Empty:* 24,000 lb.
Max. take-off weight: 43,497 lb.

PERFORMANCE

(Mk. 200).   *Service ceiling:* 28,500′.
Take-off run: 4,100′.
Range: 1,059 miles at 295 m.p.h. at 20,000′ with full payload.

The Friendship is the aircraft with which this great Dutch manufacturer re-entered the air transport market in 1955. By January 1970 a total of 529 Friendships had been ordered from Fokker and their U.S. licensees, Fairchild Hiller.

There are six commercial versions. The basic F.27 Mk. 100 and 200 airliners are similar except for their engines, as described above. The Mk. 300 and 400 Combiplanes are special cargo or mixed cargo/passenger versions of the 100 and 200 respectively, with a large side-loading door and other changes. The Series 500 is a 'stretched' version of the 200, with longer fuselage, larger cargo door and more seats. The Mk. 600 has a larger cargo door but lacks the reinforced floor of the Combiplanes.

FOKKER F.28 FELLOWSHIP Mk. 1000 (Netherlands)

First Flight: **May 9, 1967**

AIRFRAME

Low wings, swept back at 16°. Sweptback tail surfaces, with variable-incidence tailplane mounted near tip of fin. Each wing fitted with aileron, Fowler double-slotted trailing-edge flaps and five-section lift dumpers. Engines mounted on each side of rear fuselage. Tricycle undercarriage with twin wheels on each unit. Nose unit retracts forward, main units inward into fuselage.

ENGINES

Two Rolls-Royce Spey Mk. 555-15 turbofans, each rated at 9,850 lb.s.t. Fuel tanks in wings, with total capacity of 2,143–2,869 gal.

PAYLOAD

Crew of two on flight deck. Seats for 55–65 passengers, five-abreast, in main cabin, with baggage compartment, wardrobe and toilet aft of cabin. Two further freight holds under floor.

DIMENSIONS

Wing span: 77′ 4¼″.   *Length:* 89′ 10¾″.
Height: 27′ 9½″.   *Wing area:* 822 sq. ft.

WEIGHTS

Basic operating weight: 34,500 lb.
Max. take-off weight: 63,000 lb.

PERFORMANCE

Max. cruising speed: 528 m.p.h.
Max. cruising height: 30,000′.
Take-off run: 4,660′ (at 57,620 lb. weight).
Typical range: 1,266 miles at 427 m.p.h. with 60 passengers.

The Fellowship was designed as a short-range jet-liner for operators who had received good service from the F.27 Friendship. The first delivery was made to LTU of Germany in February 1969 and production of components for 40 aircraft was authorised in the spring of that year. Ten of these are going to Fairchild Hiller, the U.S. agents. Associated with Fokker-VFW in the project are Messerschmitt-Bölkow-Blohm and VFW-Fokker of Germany, and Short Brothers and Harland of Great Britain who are sharing costs and manufacturing portions of the aircraft. The Mk. 2000 version will differ in carrying 79 passengers in a longer cabin; its weight will be 65,000 lb.

HANDLEY PAGE HERALD SERIES 200 (Great Britain)

First Flight (Herald prototype): **August 25, 1955**

AIRFRAME
High unswept wings. Unswept tail surfaces, with large dorsal fin. Conventional control surfaces and slotted Fowler flaps. Tricycle undercarriage; all units with twin wheels and retracting forward.

ENGINES
Two Rolls-Royce Dart Mk. 527 turboprop engines, each rated at 2,105 h.p. and driving a four-blade reversible-pitch airscrew. Fuel tanks in wings, with capacity of 1,080 gal., may be supplemented by underwing pylon tanks.

PAYLOAD
Crew of two on flight deck. Seats for up to 56 passengers in pressurised cabin, with buffet, toilet and rear compartment for luggage and freight. Seats easily removable for freight or mixed passenger/freight operations.

DIMENSIONS
Wing span: 94′ 9″.   *Length:* 75′ 6″.
Height: 24′ 1″.   *Wing area:* 886 sq. ft.

WEIGHTS
Basic operating weight: 25,800 lb.
Max. take-off weight: 43,000 lb.

PERFORMANCE
Service ceiling: 30,000′.
Take-off distance to 35′: 2,700′ at weight of 39,500 lb.
Typical range: 425 miles at 275 m.p.h. at 15,000′ with full payload.

When the Herald was first planned in the early 1950s, it seemed as if many local-service operators were not yet ready to switch from piston-engines to turboprops; the two prototypes were, therefore, each powered originally by four 870 h.p. Leonides Major piston-engines. Subsequently, both were re-engined with Darts, the first flight with the new power plants being made on March 11, 1958.

In January 1970, about 43 Heralds were in service with 10 civil and military operators in the United Kingdom and overseas. They included seven belonging to British United Island Airways. Most production aircraft are of the Series 200 version. Court operate three ex-B.E.A. Series 100 Heralds, with 42-in. shorter fuselage.

HAWKER SIDDELEY 748 (Great Britain)
First Flight: **June 24, 1960**

AIRFRAME
Low unswept wings. Unswept tail surfaces with dorsal fin. Conventional control surfaces and Fowler flaps. Engines mounted above wings to avoid cut-outs in wing spars. Tricycle undercarriage with twin wheels on each unit. All units retract forward, main wheels into fairings below engine nacelles.

ENGINES
Two Rolls-Royce Dart Mk. 514 turboprops, each rated at 1,880 h.p. (748 Series 1), or Dart Mk. 531 turboprops, each rated at 2,105 h.p. (748 Series 2), or Dart Mk. 532–2L, rated at 2,280 h.p. (748 Series 2A), driving four-blade airscrews. Fuel tanks with total capacity of 1,140 or 1,440 gal. in wings.

PAYLOAD
Crew of two on flight deck. Seats for 40–58 passengers in pressurised cabin, with galley, toilet, baggage and freight compartments.

DIMENSIONS
Wing span: 98′ 6″.　　*Length:* 67′.
Height: 24′ 10″.
Wing area: 810.75 sq. ft.

WEIGHTS
(748 Srs. 1). *Empty:* 24,000 lb.
Max. take-off weight: 39,500 lb.
(748 Srs. 2A). *Empty:* 25,988 lb.
Max. take-off weight: 44,495 lb.

PERFORMANCE
(748 Srs. 2A). *Max. cruising speed:* 287 m.p.h.
Take-off run: 2,750′.
Typical range: 690 miles with full payload.

The H.S. 748 combines the dimensions of the veteran DC–3 with the improved payload and performance made possible by the use of turboprop engines. The first production 748 Series 1 flew on August 30, 1961, and this version is in service with Skyways, B.K.S. and Argentine Airlines, which bought three, two and 12 respectively. By early 1970 the higher-powered 748 Series 2 and 2A had been ordered by 30 commercial, government and military customers throughout the world.

The 748 is also being built in India for the Indian Air Force and airlines. A military version, with a loading ramp for vehicles under its upswept rear fuselage, is in service with the R.A.F., as the Andover Mk. 1. Andover Mk. 2s used by the R.A.F. and the Queen's Flight are similar to the 748 Series 2.

HAWKER SIDDELEY ARGOSY (Great Britain)

First Flight: **January 8, 1959**

AIRFRAME

High unswept wings. Fuselage 'pod' has sideways-hinged loading doors at nose and tail. Twin-fin tail unit is carried on twin tail-booms in line with inner engines. Conventional control surfaces and double-slotted flaps. Tricycle undercarriage with twin wheels on each unit. All units retract rearward.

ENGINES

Four Rolls-Royce Dart Mk. 532/1 turbo-props, each rated at 2,230 h.p. and driving a four-blade reversible-pitch airscrew. Fuel tanks with total capacity of 3,400 gal. in wings.

PAYLOAD

Crew of two or three on raised flight deck above freight hold. Main cabin has capacity of 3,680 cu. ft. and can carry up to 31,000 lb. of freight and vehicles and up to 89 passengers.

DIMENSIONS

Wing span: 115'. *Length:* 86' 9".
Height: 29' 3". *Wing area:* 1,458 sq. ft.

WEIGHTS

Basic operating weight: 48,680 lb.
Max. take-off weight: 93,000 lb.

PERFORMANCE

Service ceiling: 20,000'.
Typical range: 500 miles at 280 m.p.h. with max. payload.

Quick loading and unloading is the key to efficient operation of a freight-plane. For that reason, the Argosy was designed with 'straight-through' nose and tail loading doors and a built-in roller-conveyor system. Vehicles can be driven up ramps straight into either end of the cabin, which is 46 ft. 8 in. long, 10 ft. wide and 6 ft. 8 in. high. Ten Argosy Series 100 aircraft were built, of which eight now belong to Universal Airlines in the U.S.A. B.E.A. has five Series 220 Argosies, as described above, with redesigned wing which reduces the structure weight by a quarter of a ton. A military version, with 'beaver-tail' rear loading doors but no nose-door, is in service with the R.A.F.

HAWKER SIDDELEY (D.H.) COMET 4C (Great Britain)

First Flight (Comet 1 prototype): **July 27, 1949**

AIRFRAME

Low wings, swept back at 20°, with external fuel tanks mounted on leading-edges. Unswept tail surfaces. Conventional control surfaces and trailing-edge flaps. Engines buried in wing-roots. Tricycle undercarriage, with twin nose-wheels and main four-wheel bogies. Nose-wheels retract rearward. Main units retract outward into wings.

ENGINES

Four Rolls-Royce Avon RA.29 Mk. 525B turbojets, each rated at 10,500 lb.s.t. Fuel tanks in wings, centre-section and on leading-edges, with total capacity of 8,908 gal.

PAYLOAD

Crew of four on flight deck. Seats for 72–101 passengers in pressurised cabin, with galley, toilets and wardrobe. Three freight compartments at rear of cabin and under floor, with total volume of 659 cu. ft.

DIMENSIONS

Wing span: 114′ 10″. *Length:* 118′.
Height: 29′ 6″. *Wing area:* 2,121 sq. ft.

WEIGHTS

Basic operating weight: 79,600 lb.
Max. take-off weight: 162,000 lb.

PERFORMANCE

Runway length required for take-off: 6,750′.
Typical range: 2,590 miles at 542 m.p.h. at 31,000′ with 19,630-lb. payload.

Three versions of the Comet are still in airline service. The basic Comet 4 as used by Dan-Air, Mexicana, AREA, East African Airways and Argentine Airlines, was first flown on April 27, 1958, and was used by B.O.A.C. to open the world's first transatlantic jet service on October 4, 1958. It is the long-range version, and differs from the Comet 4C described above by having a shorter fuselage seating 60–81 passengers. The medium-range Comet 4B, flown by B.E.A. Airtours and Channel Airways, has the longer fuselage of the 4C, but has a wing span of only 107 ft. 10 in. and no leading-edge tanks. The inter-mediate-range 4C is operated by Mexicana, United Arab Airlines, Middle East Airlines, Argentine Airlines, Kuwait Airways and Sudan Airways, as well as by R.A.F. Transport Command. Deliveries of the Comet 4, 4B and 4C totalled 72.

HAWKER SIDDELEY (D.H.) HERON SERIES 2 (Great Britain)

First Flight (Heron Series 1): **May 10, 1950**

AIRFRAME

Low unswept wings. Unswept tail surfaces. Conventional control surfaces and trailing-edge flaps. Tricycle undercarriage, with single wheel on each unit. Nose-wheel retracts rearward, main units outward into wings between engine nacelles.

ENGINES

Four Bristol Siddeley Gipsy Queen 30 Mk. 2 six-cylinder inverted in-line air-cooled engines, each rated at 250 h.p. and driving a two-blade airscrew. Fuel tanks in wings, with capacity of 412 gal.

PAYLOAD

Crew of two on flight deck. Seats for 14–17 passengers in main cabin, with luggage compartments fore and aft of cabin and toilet on 14–15 seat versions.

DIMENSIONS

Wing span: 71′ 6″.   *Length:* 48′ 6″.
Height: 15′ 7″.   *Wing area:* 499 sq. ft.

WEIGHTS

Basic operating weight: 8,484 lb.
Max. take-off weight: 13,500 lb.

PERFORMANCE

Typical range: 915 miles at 183 m.p.h. at 8,000′ with 1,950-lb. payload.

By 'stretching' the wings and fuselage of the earlier 8/11 seat, twin-engined Dove light transport, fitting four Gipsy Queen 30 engines and a non-retractable tricycle undercarriage, de Havilland produced the original Heron Series 1, which is still giving good service with some airlines. To improve performance, a retractable undercarriage is fitted to the Heron Series 2, described above, which was the main production version.

A total of 148 Herons were built for service in more than 30 countries. Many are specially furnished as executive transports. Some have been re-engined with more powerful Continental or Lycoming horizontally-opposed engines. The Canadian Saunders ST–27, first flown on May 28, 1969, is a lengthened 24-seat Heron with two 715-h.p. United Aircraft of Canada (Pratt & Whitney) PT6A–27 turboprops.

HAWKER SIDDELEY (D.H.) TRIDENT 2E (Great Britain)

First Flight (Trident 1): **January 9, 1962**

AIRFRAME

Low wings, swept back at 35°. Sweptback tail surfaces, with tailplane mounted at top of fin. Conventional ailerons and rudder. All-moving tailplane with geared slotted flap on trailing-edge. Double-slotted trailing-edge wing flaps work in conjunction with leading-edge flaps, slats and spoiler air-brakes. Two engines mounted in pods on sides of rear fuselage. Air intake for third engine at base of fin. Tricycle undercarriage. Twin-wheel nose unit is offset to port and retracts sideways. Each main unit has two pairs of wheels side-by-side and retracts inward into fuselage.

ENGINES

Three Rolls-Royce RB 163–25 Mk. 512–5W Spey turbofans, each rated at 11,930 lb.s.t. Fuel tanks in wings and centre-section with capacity of 6,400 gal.

PAYLOAD

Crew of three on flight deck. Seats for 91–149 passengers in pressurised cabin, with galleys, toilets and coat stowage. Space for 760 cu. ft. of luggage and freight in underfloor holds.

DIMENSIONS

Wing span: 98′.   *Length:* 114′ 9″.
Height: 27′.   *Wing area:* 1,461 sq. ft.

WEIGHTS

Basic operating weight: 73,200 lb.
Max. take-off weight: 143,500 lb.

PERFORMANCE

Max. cruising speed: 605 m.p.h.
Take-off run: 6,400′.
Typical range: 2,430 miles at 596 m.p.h. at 30,000′ with full payload.

First of the 'second-generation' British jet liners, the Trident followed the Comet into service with B.E.A. in March 1964. Twenty-four Trident 1s, with 9,850 lb.s.t. Speys and span of 89′ 10″, were delivered to this airline which also has 15 Trident 2s, as described and illustrated, and has ordered 26 Trident 3s, with longer fuselage for 128–179 passengers and a Rolls-Royce RB.162 turbojet in the tail for improved take-off performance. Cyprus Airways has two Trident 2s. The Trident 1E with 11,400 lb. Speys, span of 95′ and 115–139 seats, was delivered to Air Ceylon (1), BKS (2), Channel Airways (2), Iraqi Airways (3), Kuwait Airways (3) and Pakistan International Airlines (4).

ILYUSHIN Il–14 (Russia) and AVIA–14 (Czechoslovakia)
First Flight (Il–14): **1953**

AIRFRAME

Low unswept wings. Unswept tail surfaces. Conventional control surfaces and trailing-edge slotted flaps. Tricycle undercarriage, with single rearward-retracting nose-wheel and forward-retracting twin-wheel main units.

ENGINES

Two Shvetsov ASh–82T fourteen-cylinder two-row radial engines, each rated at 1,900 h.p. and driving a four-blade airscrew. Fuel tanks in wings, with capacity of 770 gal. Avia–14 Salon can be fitted with tip-tanks, giving max. capacity of 946 gal.

PAYLOAD

Flight crew of three or four. Passenger accommodation varies according to type, as described below.

DIMENSIONS

(Avia 14 Salon). *Wing span:* 106′ 8″.
Length: 73′ 2″.
Height: 25′ 7″.   *Wing area:* 1,076 sq. ft.

WEIGHTS

(Avia–14 Salon). *Empty:* 27,670 lb.
Max. take-off weight: 39,683 lb.

PERFORMANCE

(Avia–14 Salon). *Max. speed:* 249 m.p.h.
Take-off run: 1,900′.
Typical range: 280 miles at 186 m.p.h. at 6,500′ with full payload.

The basic Il–14 was put into very large-scale production in the Soviet Union in two forms. The Il–14P seats 18–26 passengers; the Il–14M has a longer fuselage and seats 24–28 passengers, with galley, toilet and luggage hold. Licence production of the Il–14P was undertaken in the VEB Flugzeugbau at Dresden in East Germany, the first German-built example flying in April 1956. A further production line was set up in Czechoslovakia, where the design was re-stressed to ICAO standards to permit operation at a greater all-up weight, and re-designated the Avia 14–32. This had accommodation for 32 passengers, and was followed by the further improved 36/42-seat Avia–14 Salon, described above and illustrated opposite.

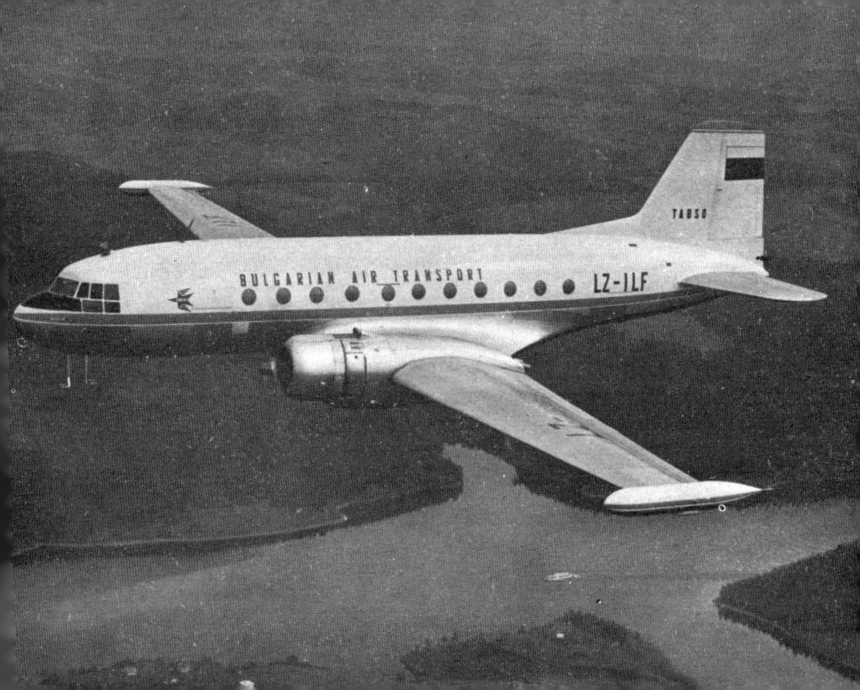
BULGARIAN AIR TRANSPORT
LZ-ILF
TABSO

ILYUSHIN Il–18V (Russia)
First Flight: **July, 1957**

AIRFRAME
Low unswept wings. Unswept tail surfaces. Conventional control surfaces and double-slotted flaps. Tricycle undercarriage, with twin nose-wheels and four-wheel bogie on each main unit. All units retract forward, main wheels into inner engine nacelles.

ENGINES
Four Ivchenko AI–20K turboprops, each rated at 4,000 h.p. and driving a four-blade reversible-pitch airscrew. Fuel tanks in wings, with total capacity of 5,213 gal.

PAYLOAD
Crew of five on flight deck. Standard seating for 90–122 passengers in three separate cabins in pressurised fuselage. Two wardrobes and toilets forward of cabins; galley and two toilets aft. Three cargo compartments with total volume of 1,035 cu. ft.

DIMENSIONS
Wing span: 122′ 8½″.   *Length:* 117′ 9″.
Height: 33′ 4″.   *Wing area:* 1,507 sq. ft.

WEIGHTS
Basic operating weight: 76,000 lb.
Max. take-off weight: 134,925 lb.

PERFORMANCE
Max. cruising speed: 404 m.p.h.
Take-off run: 3,940′.
Typical range: 1,550 miles at 373 m.p.h. at 25,000′ with full payload.

In much the same class as the Vanguard and Electra, this elegant turboprop airliner has been in regular service with Aeroflot since April 1959 and has been supplied to 13 other airlines, including those of Hungary, East Germany, Czechoslovakia, Rumania, Bulgaria, Cuba, Egypt, Guinea, Mali, Poland and China. In common with many contemporary Soviet airliners and unlike most Western transports, its flying controls are operated manually and not through electrically or hydraulically powered control systems. Equipment includes weather radar, instrument landing system, automatic navigation aids, automatic radio-compasses and a radio altimeter.

In addition to the original Il-18V, described and illustrated, there are two versions with 4,250 h.p. AI–20M engines—the 110/122-seat Il-18E and the Il-18D with extra fuel and take-off weight of 141,100 lb.

ILYUSHIN Il-62 (Russia)

First Flight: **January, 1963**

AIRFRAME

Low wings, swept back at 35°, with fixed leading-edge droop on 'dogtooth' outer panels. Each wing fitted with three-section aileron, double-slotted flaps and two spoilers. Sweptback tail surfaces, with tailplane mounted at tip of fin. Engines mounted in lateral pairs on each side of rear fuselage. Tricycle undercarriage, with twin nose-wheels and inward-retracting main four-wheel bogies.

ENGINES

Four Kuznetsov NK–8–4 turbofans, each rated at 23,150 lb.s.t. Seven fuel tanks in wings, capacity 21,998 gal.

PAYLOAD

Pressurised cabin for 114–186 passengers six-abreast in standard form or 85 passengers in first class/de luxe layout, including 40 sleeperette chairs, five toilets, galley and wardrobes. Freight holds under floor and in rear fuselage with total capacity of 1,585 cu. ft.

DIMENSIONS

Wing span: 141' 9". *Length:* 174' 3½".
Height: 40' 6¼". *Wing area:* 3,010 sq. ft.

WEIGHTS

Basic operating weight: 153,000 lb.
Max. take-off weight: 357,000 lb.

PERFORMANCE

Normal cruising speed: 528–560 m.p.h.
Take-off run: 5,905'.
Range: 4,160 miles with max. payload;
5,715 miles with max. fuel.

Announced on September 24, 1962, the Il-62 is a long-range jet airliner which has been developed to replace the turboprop Tu–114 in service with Aeroflot. Its layout is very like that of the BAC Super VC10 and the two aircraft are in much the same class. For the first two years, the prototypes were flight tested with Lyulka turbojets of only 16,535 lb.s.t., as the Kuznetsov turbofans were not ready. A production Il-62 replaced the Tu–114 on Aeroflot's Moscow-Montreal transatlantic service in September 1967, and inaugurated the airline's New York service in the following July. It is used on many other long Aeroflot routes and three have been bought by CSA Czech Airlines.

LOCKHEED L-1049G SUPER CONSTELLATION (U.S.A.)

First Flight (C–69 Constellation): **January 9, 1943**

AIRFRAME

Low unswept wings. Unswept tail surfaces, with three fins and two rudders. Conventional control surfaces and Fowler flaps. Tricycle undercarriage with twin wheels on all units. Nose-wheels retract rearward, main units forward.

ENGINES

Four Wright R–3350–CA18–EA3 or EA6 Turbo Compound eighteen-cylinder two-row radial engines, each rated at 3,400 h.p. and driving a three-blade reversible-pitch airscrew. Total of 6,453 gal. of fuel in wings and wingtip tanks.

PAYLOAD

Crew of four on flight deck. Seats for 65–99 passengers in pressurised cabin, with galley, toilets, cloakroom and two underfloor baggage and freight compartments with volume of 728 cu. ft.

DIMENSIONS

Wing span: 123'.   *Length:* 113' 7".
Height: 24' 9".   *Wing area:* 1,650 sq. ft.

WEIGHTS

Empty: 73,016 lb.
Max. take-off weight: 137,500 lb.

PERFORMANCE

Max. speed: 376 m.p.h.
Typical range: 4,810 miles at 280 m.p.h. at 20,000' with 18,315-lb. payload.

Like the DC–4, the original Constellation was under development pre-war for airline use, but was taken over as a military transport, under the designation C–69, before entering commercial service. After the war, the first Model 049 Constellation airliners were assembled from C–69 components. They were 43-seaters, with 2,200 h.p. Wright Cyclone engines, length of 95 ft. 1 in. and take-off weight of 86,250 lb. Changes such as the use of more powerful Cyclones and increased fuel tankage produced the later Models 149, 649A, 749 and 749A. Then, on October 13, 1950, Lockheed flew the prototype of the Model 1049 Super Constellation, with 2,800 h.p. Cyclones and an 18 ft. 6 in. longer fuselage, seating up to 92 passengers. A switch to Turbo Compound engines produced the Model 1049C, the strengthened 1049E, the 1049G (described above), and the 1049D and 1049H cargo versions. Several Constellations and Super Constellations remain in service, mainly for freight carrying, together with a few L–1649A Starliners with square-tip wings spanning 150'.

LOCKHEED L–188A ELECTRA (U.S.A.)

First Flight: **December 6, 1957**

AIRFRAME

Low unswept wings. Unswept tail surfaces, with dihedral on tailplane and a large dorsal fin. Conventional control surfaces and Fowler flaps. Tricycle undercarriage, with twin wheels on each unit. All wheels retract forward, main units into inner engine nacelles.

ENGINES

Four Allison 501–D13 turboprops, each rated at 3,750 h.p. and driving a four-blade reversible-pitch airscrew. Fuel tanks in wings, with capacity of 4,600 or 5,435 gal.

PAYLOAD

Crew of up to five on flight deck. Seats for 44–99 passengers in pressurised cabin, with toilets and galley. Total of 636 cu. ft. of space for luggage and freight in main cabin and under floor.

DIMENSIONS

Wing span: 99'. *Length:* 104' 6½".
Height: 32' 1". *Wing area:* 1,300 sq. ft.

WEIGHTS

Basic operating weight: 57,300 lb.
Max. take-off weight: 116,000 lb.

PERFORMANCE

Max. speed: 448 m.p.h.
Service ceiling: 28,400'.
Take-off run: 4,720'.
Typical range: 2,500 miles at 380 m.p.h. at 22,000' with 22,000-lb. payload.

First U.S. turboprop airliner to enter regular service, the Electra was produced mainly to meet the requirements of U.S. domestic operators. A total of 162 were bought by fourteen airlines, the largest foreign order being 12 for K.L.M. Deliveries were completed in 1961, and most Electras have now been sold to smaller airlines, following their replacement by jets. However, Lockheed have since produced in large numbers an anti-submarine development of the Electra known as the P–3 Orion. This has a redesigned fuselage, with bomb-bay, magnetic anomaly detection (MAD) search gear in a long tail 'sting' and other extensive equipment to detect and destroy submarines.

MIL Mi-4 (Russia)

First Flight: **Probably 1952**

AIRFRAME

Conventional 'single-rotor' layout. Pod-and-boom fuselage, with three-blade tail anti-torque rotor at end of cranked tailboom. Four-blade main rotor, driven by engine mounted in nose. Non-retractable four-wheel undercarriage, often with spats on wheels.

ENGINES

One Shvetsov ASh-82V eighteen-cylinder two-row radial engine, rated at 1,700 h.p.

PAYLOAD

Crew of two on flight deck. Main cabin seats 8–16 passengers, with toilet, wardrobe and compartment for 220 lb. of baggage at rear. Ambulance version carries eight stretchers and attendant. Freighter has clam-shell rear doors.

DIMENSIONS

Main rotor diameter: 68′ 11″.
Length: 55′ 1″.   *Height:* 17′.

WEIGHTS

Max. payload: 3,835 lb.
Max. take-off weight: 17,200 lb.

PERFORMANCE

Max. speed: 130 m.p.h.
Service ceiling: 18,000′.
Typical range: 155 miles at 99 m.p.h. at 5,000′ with 11 passengers and 220 lb. of baggage.

Standard medium-size helicopter in service with Aeroflot and the Soviet armed forces for many years, the Mi-4 has also been exported to many foreign countries. It is a highly efficient aircraft and set up an internationally recognised height-with-payload record, which involved lifting a payload of about two tons to a height of 19,744 ft.

Variants of the Mi-4 are used for many duties beside helicopter passenger services. In particular, there is an agricultural version, the Mi-4S, with a container for nearly a ton of chemicals in its cabin and spray-bars extending on each side of the fuselage. Radio and instruments for night and bad weather flying are standard equipment.

MIL Mi–8 (Russia)
First Flight: **Probably 1961**

AIRFRAME
Conventional 'single-rotor' layout. Pod-and-boom fuselage, with three-blade tail anti-torque rotor at end of cranked tail-boom. Five-blade main rotor, driven by two turbine engines mounted side-by-side above cabin. Non-retractable tricycle undercarriage, with twin nose-wheels and single wheel on each main unit. Main wheels can be spatted.

ENGINES
Two Isotov TB–2–117A shaft-turbines, each rated at 1,500 h.p. Single fuel tank in fuselage and two external tanks, on each side of cabin, with total capacity of 3,196 lb.

PAYLOAD
Crew of two side-by-side in nose. Main cabin accommodates 28 passengers four-abreast or 12 stretchers and attendant in ambulance role. Wardrobe, toilet and baggage compartment standard. Cabin can be stripped for freight carrying.

DIMENSIONS
Main rotor diameter: 69′ 10¼″.
Length: 60′ 0¾″.   *Height:* 18′ 4½″.

WEIGHTS
Basic operating weight: 16,352 lb.
Max. take-off weight: 26,455 lb.

PERFORMANCE
Max. speed: 155 m.p.h.
Service ceiling: 14,760′.
Range: 223 miles at 112 m.p.h. with max. payload.

By switching to turbine power, with the engines mounted above the cabin, Mil was able to produce a transport helicopter with twice the payload of the Mi–4, without any great increase in overall dimensions. When first seen at the 1961 Tushino Air Display, the Mi–8 (known also as the V–8) had a single, larger shaft-turbine and four-blade main rotor; but the twin-engine version, with five-blade rotor, is now standard. The Mi–8 set up two officially recognised records, for a speed of 125.41 m.p.h. around a 1,243-mile (2,000 km.) circuit and a closed-circuit distance record of 1,532 miles. It is in large-scale production for both civil and military use, and in standard service with Aeroflot and the Soviet Armed Forces, and has been exported to other countries.

NAMC YS–11–100 (Japan)

First Flight: **August 30, 1962**

AIRFRAME

Low unswept wings. Unswept tail surfaces with dorsal fin. Conventional control surfaces and Fowler flaps. Engines mounted above wings to avoid cut-outs in spars. Tricycle undercarriage with twin wheels on each unit. All units retract forward, main wheels into fairings below engine nacelles.

ENGINES

Two Rolls-Royce Dart Mk. 542–10 turboprops, each rated at 3,060 h.p., driving four-blade airscrews. Fuel tanks in wings, with total capacity of 1,600 gal.

PAYLOAD

Crew of two on flight deck. Seats for 52–60 passengers in pressurised cabin, with galley and toilets. Baggage compartments forward of cabin and under floor. Freight hold aft of cabin.

DIMENSIONS

Wing span: 104′ 11¾″. *Length:* 86′ 3½″. *Height:* 29′ 5¾″. *Wing area:* 1,020 sq. ft.

WEIGHTS

Basic operating weight: 33,290 lb.
Max. take-off weight: 51,800 lb.

PERFORMANCE

Max. cruising speed: 297 m.p.h. at 15,000′
Service ceiling: 27,500′.
Take-off run: 3,180′.
Range: 860 miles at 292 m.p.h. at 20,000′ with max. payload.

The YS-11 is being produced under a national transport aircraft programme, in which most of the major Japanese aircraft manufacturers are participating. For example, Mitsubishi is producing fuselages and equipment, Kawasaki the wings and Fuji the tail unit. Nihon Aeroplane Manufacturing Company (NAMC), run co-operatively by the government and industry, is responsible for design, supervision of the programme and sales. Mitsubishi handles final assembly and flight testing.

In addition to the basic YS-11-100 (described and illustrated), there are three new models with increased take-off weight—the 60-passenger YS-11A-200, with payload increased by 2,970 lb. and max. weight of 54,010 lb., which is the standard current production version, the YS-11A-300 passenger/freighter carrying 46 passengers, and the all cargo YS-11A-400. 128 YS-11s had been sold by early 1970.

NORD/AEROSPATIALE 262 Series A (France)

First Flight: **December 24, 1962**

AIRFRAME
High unswept wings. Unswept tail surfaces with dorsal fin. Conventional control surfaces, with slotted ailerons and flaps. Tricycle undercarriage, with single wheel on each unit. Main wheels retract upward into fairings on sides of fuselage.

ENGINES
Two Turboméca Bastan VI.C turboprops, each rated at 1,065 h.p. and driving a three-blade airscrew. Fuel tanks in wings, with total capacity of 450 or 579 gal.

PAYLOAD
Crew of two on flight deck. Pressurised cabin seating 26–29 passengers, with toilet and coat space at rear. Movable bulkhead permits mixed cargo/passenger operation. Freight holds forward of cabin, with normal capacity of 159 cu. ft.

DIMENSIONS
Wing span: 71′ 10″.　　*Length:* 63′ 3″.
Height: 20′ 4″.　　*Wing area:* 592 sq. ft.

WEIGHTS
Basic operating weight: 15,496 lb.
Max. take-off weight: 23,369 lb.

PERFORMANCE
Max. speed: 239 m.p.h.
Service ceiling: 19,200′.
Take-off run: 3,100′.
Typical range: 565 miles at 233 m.p.h. with max. payload.

Development of this twin-engined light transport was undertaken initially by the Max Holste company, now Reims Aviation, who built the prototype MH.250 Super Broussard, with 600 h.p. Pratt & Whitney R–1340 piston-engines. Production was taken over by Nord-Aviation, who built first a small series of similar aircraft, but with turboprop engines, under the designation MH.260. These were superseded in production by the Series A Nord 262, as described above, with a new pressurised fuselage of circular cross-section. Latest version is the Series C with 1,130 h.p. Bastan VII.A engines and improved performance. By 1970, total civil and military orders were approaching 100, the biggest commercial contract being 12 for Allegheny Airlines, U.S.A.

SHORT SC.7 SKYVAN Series 3 (Great Britain)

First Flight (Piston-engined Skyvan): **January 17, 1963**

AIRFRAME

High unswept wings, with single bracing strut each side. Unswept tail surfaces, with twin rectangular fins and rudders carried at tips of tailplane. Snub-nosed square-section fuselage, with loading-ramp under upswept rear portion. Non-retractable tricycle undercarriage, with single wheel on each unit.

ENGINES

Two AiResearch TPE 331–201 turboprops, each rated at 715 h.p. and driving a three-blade airscrew. Fuel tanks in top of fuselage between wings, with total capacity of 293 gal.

PAYLOAD

Crew of one or two on flight deck. Can carry 19 passengers, 12 stretcher patients and attendants, or 4,600 lb. of freight or vehicles in main cabin.

DIMENSIONS

Wing span: 64′ 11″.   *Length:* 40′ 1″.
Height: 15′ 1″.   *Wing area:* 373 sq. ft.

WEIGHTS

Basic operating weight: 7,289 lb.
Max. take-off weight: 12,500 lb.

PERFORMANCE

Max. cruising speed: 201 m.p.h.
Service ceiling: 22,500′.
Take-off run: 850′–1,680′.
Typical range: 306 miles at 173 m.p.h. at 10,000′ with 4,000-lb. payload.

Short Brothers & Harland of Belfast developed this light utility transport as a private venture, with particular emphasis on easy loading, simple maintenance and good performance in under-developed areas. The prototype was flown initially with 390 h.p. Continental piston-engines. It was soon re-engined with Astazou II turboprops and flew for the first time in this form on October 2, 1963. Manufacture of a small initial quantity of Series 2 Skyvans, with Astazou XII engines, has been followed by series production of the Series 3, as described and illustrated. An executive version is available, with 9 seats in a de luxe cabin, with cocktail cabinet, desk and galley.

SIKORSKY S–58 (U.S.A.)
First Flight: **March 8, 1954**

AIRFRAME

Unlike most ' single-rotor ' helicopters, the S–58 has a proper rear fuselage instead of the usual pod-and-boom layout. The tail rotor is carried at the top of a stabilising fin and there is a small tailplane. Main and tail rotors are each four-bladed. Non-retractable tail-wheel undercarriage, with single wheel on each unit.

ENGINES

One Wright R–1820–84 nine-cylinder radial engine, rated at 1,525 h.p., mounted behind clam-shell doors in the fuselage nose. Fuel tank capacity varies from 165 to 256 gal.

PAYLOAD

Crew of two on flight deck. Seats in main cabin for 12–18 passengers, or fittings for eight stretchers.

DIMENSIONS

Main rotor diameter: 56'.
Length: 46' 9"   *Height:* 15' 11".

WEIGHTS

Empty: 7,675 lb.
Max. take-off weight: 13,000 lb.

PERFORMANCE

Max. speed: 123 m.p.h.
Service ceiling: 9,000'.
Max. range: 280 miles at 98 m.p.h. at 5,000'.

A total of 1,821 S–58 type helicopters were built, which is more than any other Sikorsky design. Most are in military use, as the U.S. Army uses the CH–34 Choctaw version as a standard military general-purpose transport, while the U.S. Navy uses the SH–34J Seabat version for anti-submarine duties and the U.S. Marine Corps uses the UH–34 Seahorse as an assault transport. However, quite a number have gone into commercial service with helicopter airlines such as Chicago Helicopter Airways. Others are used widely for freight-carrying. Turbine-powered versions are being manufactured by Westland, in England, under the name Wessex.

SIKORSKY S–61N (U.S.A.)

First Flight (S–61L): **December 6, 1960**

AIRFRAME

Fuselage is similar in appearance to the hull of a flying-boat and is sealed for operation off water. The engines are mounted above the main cabin. Main and tail rotors are both five-bladed. Tail-wheel undercarriage, with twin-wheel main units which retract into stabilising floats and single non-retractable tail-wheel.

ENGINES

Two General Electric CT58–140–2 shaft-turbines, each rated at 1,500 h.p. Fuel tanks in hull with capacity of 341–545 gal.

PAYLOAD

Crew of two on flight deck. Seats in cabin for 30 passengers, or 25 passengers with galley and toilet. 150 cu. ft. of baggage space. Alternative layout for mixed passenger/freight services.

DIMENSIONS

Main rotor diameter: 62'.
Length: 72' 10".   *Height:* 18' 5¼".

WEIGHTS

Basic operating weight: 12,256 lb.
Max. take-off weight: 19,000 lb.

PERFORMANCE

Max. speed: 150 m.p.h.
Service ceiling: 12,500'.
Typical range: 460 miles at 140 m.p.h. at 5,000' with maximum fuel.

Although the S–61 is basically a commercial counterpart of the U.S. Navy's amphibious SH–3 Sea King anti-submarine helicopter, the version in service with Los Angeles Airways is non-amphibious. Instead, the hull contains two large roll-out 'drawers' for baggage.

This version is known as the S–61L. The other, as described and illustrated, is the fully amphibious S–61N. This is operated by B.E.A., who fly S–61Ns on their service to the Isles of Scilly, and many other companies, mostly in small numbers so that total production was still under 50 by early 1970. Early models had 1,250 h.p. CT58–110 engines.

SUD-AVIATION/AEROSPATIALE S.E.210 CARAVELLE VI-R
(France)

First Flight (Caravelle Prototype): **May 27, 1955**

AIRFRAME

Low wings, swept back at 20°. Sweptback tail surfaces, with tailplane mounted partway up fin. Wings fitted with two-piece ailerons, slotted flaps, air-brakes ahead of flaps and (on Caravelle VI-R, 10R and 11R) three-section spoilers on trailing-edges. Engines mounted in pods on sides of rear fuselage. Tricycle undercarriage, with twin wheels on nose unit and four-wheel bogie main units. Nose-wheels retract forward, main wheels inward.

ENGINES

Two Rolls-Royce Avon 533R turbojets, each rated at 12,600 lb.s.t. Fuel tanks in wings, with capacity of 4,180 gal.

PAYLOAD

Crew of two or three on flight deck. Seats for 64-80 passengers in main pressurised cabin, with two galleys, toilets, coat-room and three baggage compartments with total capacity of 914 cu. ft.

DIMENSIONS

Wing span: 112′ 6″.   *Length:* 105′.
Height: 28′ 7″.   *Wing area:* 1,579 sq. ft.

WEIGHTS

Basic operating weight: 63,175 lb.
Max. take-off weight: 110,230 lb.

PERFORMANCE

Max. cruising speed: 525 m.p.h. at 25,000′.
Take-off run: 6,800′.
Range: 1,590 miles at 488 m.p.h. at 35,000′ with 16,800 lb. payload.

A completely new fashion in airliner design was set by the Caravelle, when it appeared with its engines mounted on the sides of the rear fuselage.

By early 1970, a total of 270 Caravelles had been ordered. The original Caravelle I had 10,500 lb.s.t. Avon 522 engines, and was followed by the Caravelle III with 11,400 lb.s.t. Avon 527s, the Caravelle VI-N with 12,200 lb.s.t. Avon 531s, and the Caravelle VI-R as described above, the 'R' indicating that it is fitted with thrust reversers to shorten its landing run. The Caravelle 10R differs from the VI-R in having 14,000 lb.s.t. JT8D-7 turbofans. These engines also power the Super Caravelle, which is 3 ft. 3½ in. longer, enabling up to 104 passengers to be carried. The Caravelle 11R is a passenger-freight version of the 10R. Latest version is the Caravelle 12, with 14,500 lb.s.t. JT8D-9 engines and lengthened to 118′ 10″ to accommodate 128 passengers.

TUPOLEV Tu-104A (Russia)

First Flight: **Early in 1955**

AIRFRAME

Low wings, swept back at 40° 30′ near the fuselage and at 37° 30′ outboard. Sweptback tail surfaces. Conventional control surfaces, and Fowler-type slotted flaps. Engines in nacelles at wing-roots. Tricycle undercarriage, with twin nose-wheels and main four-wheel bogies. All units retract rearward, main units into fairings built on to wing trailing-edges.

ENGINES

Two Mikulin AM-3M-500 turbojets, each rated at 21,385 lb.s.t. Fuel tanks in wings, with optional long-range tanks in fuselage, giving maximum capacity of 7,292 gal.

PAYLOAD

Crew of four on flight deck, with navigator in glazed nose compartment. Seats for 70-100 passengers in pressurised cabin, with galley, toilets and cloakroom. Freight compartments have volume of 530 cu. ft.

DIMENSIONS

Wing span: 113′ 4″.   *Length:* 126′ 4″.
Height: 39′ 4½″. *Wing area:* 1,830 sq. ft.

WEIGHTS

Basic operating weight: 91,710 lb.
Max. take-off weight: 167,450 lb.

PERFORMANCE

Max. speed: 620 m.p.h.
Service ceiling: 37,750′.
Max. range: 2,610 miles at 497 m.p.h. at 30,000′ with 17,640-lb. payload.

Most of us had our first close look at a modern Soviet aircraft when a Tu-104 jet-liner visited London Airport in 1956. The original 50-passenger version entered regular service with Aeroflot on September 15 that year and was thus the world's second jet transport, preceded only by the Comet 1. It was soon followed by the Tu-104A, as described above, which entered service in 1958, and by the 4-ft. longer Tu-104B with seating for 100 passengers, which entered service on Aeroflot's domestic routes inside Russia in the Spring of 1959. Subsequently, some Aeroflot Tu-104As were converted into 100-seaters, without lengthening the fuselage, and were redesignated Tu-104V. At least 150 Tu-104s of all types were delivered to Aeroflot and five were sold to Czechoslovakia.

The Tu-104 has the same wings, engines, undercarriage and tail unit as the Tu-1 twin-jet bomber.

TUPOLEV Tu-114 (Russia)
First Flight: **Late in 1957**

AIRFRAME
Low wings, swept back at 35°. Sweptback tail surfaces, with adjustable tailplane incidence. Conventional control surfaces, with spoilers in top surface of wings forward of ailerons. Fowler-type flaps. Tricycle undercarriage, with twin nose-wheels and main four-wheel bogies. All units retract rearward, main units into fairings built on to wing trailing-edges in line with inner engines.

ENGINES
Four Kuznetsov NK-12MV turboprops, each rated at 14,795 h.p. and driving two four-blade contra-rotating reversible-pitch airscrews. Fuel in wing tanks, with total capacity of 16,540 gal.

PAYLOAD
Flight and cabin crew of ten to fifteen. Seats for 120, 170 or 220 passengers in pressurised fuselage, depending on stage length to be flown. Galley with below-deck kitchen, cloakrooms, toilets and 48-seat restaurant cabin. Underfloor freight and baggage holds with capacity of 2,472 cu. ft.

DIMENSIONS
Wing span: 167′ 8″.   *Length:* 177′ 6″.
Height: 38′ 8½″.   *Wing area:* 3,349 sq. ft.

WEIGHTS
Basic operating weight: 200,620 lb.
Max. take-off weight: 376,990 lb.

PERFORMANCE
Max. speed: 540 m.p.h.
Service ceiling: 39,370′.
Take-off run: 8,200′.
Range: 3,850 miles at 478 m.p.h. at 29,500′ with max. payload.

The Russians have always liked to build big aeroplanes, and the Tu-114 was the largest airliner in the world when they completed it in time to mark the 40th anniversary of the Russian Revolution. Subsequently, it went into limited production and entered service with Aeroflot on April 24, 1961.

As well as being big, the Tu-114 is also the fastest turboprop airliner, with a top speed 100 m.p.h. faster than it was believed a propeller-driven airliner could fly. It holds 31 official records, among them a speed record of 545 m.p.h. around a 3,100-mile circuit, carrying a payload of 25 tons.

The Tu-114 uses the wings, tail unit, undercarriage, engines and other components of the Tu-20 long-range bomber.

TUPOLEV Tu–124V (Russia)

First Flight: **June, 1960**

AIRFRAME

Low wings, swept back at 35°. Conventional control surfaces and double-slotted flaps. Spoiler/air-brakes forward of flaps. Large air-brake under fuselage. Engines in wing-root nacelles. Tricycle undercarriage, with twin nose-wheels and main four-wheel bogies. All units retract rearward, main units into fairings built on to wing trailing-edges.

ENGINES

Two Soloviev D–20P turbofan engines, each rated at 11,905 lb.s.t. Fuel tanks in wings, capacity 2,970 gal.

PAYLOAD

Crew of three on flight deck, with provision for radio operator. Seats for 56 passengers in pressurised cabin, with buffet and baggage compartment at front, and toilet and second baggage compartment at rear.

DIMENSIONS

Wing span: 83′ 9½″. *Length:* 100′ 3½″.
Height: 26′ 6″. *Wing area:* 1,281 sq. ft.

WEIGHTS

Basic operating weight: 49,600 lb.
Max. take-off weight: 83,775 lb.

PERFORMANCE

Max. speed: 603 m.p.h.
Take-off run: 3,380′.
Max. range: 1,305 miles at 497 m.p.h. a 30,000′, with 7,715 lb. payload.

First displayed early in 1960, the Tu-124 a scaled-down development of the Tu-10 designed to provide high-speed services o Aeroflot's short and medium routes. It wa the first Soviet aircraft known to be powere by turbofan engines, which are more efficie than turbojets, giving greater range.

The original 44-seat Tu-124 entered regula service with Aeroflot in 1962. It has bee followed by the standard 56-seat Tu-124 (as described above), and two de luxe version the 36-seat Tu-124K and 22-seat Tu-124K. Three have been exported to CSA Czec Airlines.

TUPOLEV Tu–134 (Russia)

First Flight: **Probably 1964**

AIRFRAME
Low wings, swept back at 35°. Sweptback tail surfaces, with variable-incidence tailplane mounted at tip of fin. Conventional control surfaces, and double-slotted flaps. Large air-brake under fuselage. Spoilers in wings. Tricycle undercarriage, with twin nose-wheels and main four-wheel bogies. All units retract rearward, main units into fairings built on to wing trailing-edges.

ENGINES
Two Soloviev D–30 turbofans, each rated at 14,990 lb.s.t. Fuel tanks in wings with total capacity of 3,630 gal.

PAYLOAD
Crew of three on flight deck, with provision for radio operator. Seats for up to 72 four-abreast passengers in two pressurised cabins. Two galleys and baggage compartment forward of cabins. Two toilets and a large freight compartment aft of cabins.

DIMENSIONS
Wing span: 95′ 1¾″.   *Length:* 112′ 6½″.
Height: 29′ 7″.   *Wing area:* 1,370 sq. ft.

WEIGHTS
Basic operating weight: 60,627 lb.
Max. take-off weight: 98,105 lb.

PERFORMANCE
Max. cruising speed: 540 m.p.h.
Service ceiling: 41,000′.
Take-off run: 3,280′.
Range: 1,490 miles at 528 m.p.h. at 36,000′ with 15,430-lb. payload.

Russia's counterpart to the BAC One-Eleven and Douglas DC–9, the Tu–134 is a rear-engined development of the Tu–124 (see page 112). The forward fuselage has been lengthened to compensate for repositioning of the engines on the sides of the rear fuselage. The tailplane has been moved to the top of the fin. The Tu–134 entered service with Aeroflot in September 1967, and has been exported to East Germany, Bulgaria, Poland, Hungary and Yugoslavia. The developed TU–134A is 9′ 5½″ longer, providing room for 72–80 passengers and increased baggage space. It also has thrust reversers on the engines and improved electronics.

TUPOLEV Tu–144 (Russia)

First Flight: **December 31, 1968**

AIRFRAME
Low-set wings of 'double-delta' shape, with conical camber on highly-swept inner panels. Control surfaces consist of four separate elevons on each wing and a two-section rudder. No tailplane. Engines mounted in large ducts under wings. Tricycle undercarriage, with rearward-retracting twin-wheel nose unit and forward-retracting main bogies, each with three rows of four wheels.

ENGINES
Four Kuznetsov NK–144 turbofans, each rated at 28,660 lb.s.t. dry or 38,580 lb.s.t. with reheat. Capacity for 154,325 lb. of fuel.

PAYLOAD
Flight crew of three (four on prototypes). Main cabin will accommodate 100–121 passengers. Mixed-class version will have 18-seat three-abreast first-class cabin and rear tourist-class cabin with 70 five-abreast and 12 four-abreast seats. Toilet, wardrobe and baggage compartments aft of flight deck. Galley between cabins. Main baggage and freight compartment aft of passenger cabins.

DIMENSIONS
Wing span: 88' 7".   *Length: 196' 10".*

WEIGHT
Max. take-off weight: 330,000 lb.

PERFORMANCE
Max. cruising speed: 1,550 m.p.h. at 65,000'.
Take-off run: 6,235' at weight of 286,600 lb.
Typical range: 4,040 miles with 121 passengers at max. cruising speed.

Russia's counterpart to the Concorde, which flew on the last day of 1968, was the first supersonic airliner in the world to fly. Only one prototype had been completed by the spring of 1970, and the Tu–144 is not expected to enter service until 1972–73, just before the Concorde. The external shape of the two aircraft is very similar, with the same kind of drooping nose to give the pilot a better view during landing. Before the prototype flew, its aerodynamics had been flight tested in miniature by a MiG–21 fighter rebuilt with a delta wing shaped like that of the Tu–144.

116

TUPOLEV Tu–154 (Russia)

First Flight: **October 4, 1968**

AIRFRAME

Low wings, swept back at 35°. Sweptback tail surfaces, with variable-incidence tailplane mounted at tip of fin. Each wing fitted with aileron, triple-slotted trailing-edge flaps, five-section leading-edge slat and four-section spoilers, which serve as both air-brakes and lift dumpers. Two engines mounted in pods on sides of rear fuselage. Air intake for third engine at base of fin. Tricycle undercarriage, with twin-wheel nose unit. Six-wheel bogie main units retract rearward into fairings built on to wing trailing-edges.

ENGINES

Three Kuznetsov NK–8–2 turbofans, each rated at 20,950 lb.s.t. Fuel capacity 9,050–10,300 gal.

PAYLOAD

Crew of three on flight deck. Seats in pressurised main cabin for 128, 158 or 146 passengers, basically in six-abreast rows, with toilet at the front, midships galley and three toilets at rear. All-cargo version is available.

DIMENSIONS

Wing span: 123′ 2½″. *Length:* 157′ 1¾″.
Height: 37′ 4¾″. *Wing area:* 2,169 sq. ft.

WEIGHTS

Basic operating weight: 95,900 lb.
Max. take-off weight: 198,416 lb.

PERFORMANCE

Max. speed: 621 m.p.h.
Typical range: 1,565 miles at 560 m.p.h.
with maximum payload.

First flown on October 4, 1968, this fine three-engined medium/long-range transport is intended to replace the Tu–104, Il–18 and An–10 aircraft that have formed the backbone of the Aeroflot fleet for many years. It was scheduled to enter service in 1970 and will be operated by other airlines, including Czech Airlines. Max. range is up to 4,287 miles at 528 m.p.h. Developed versions already planned include a 250-seater.

VICKERS VISCOUNT (Great Britain)

First Flight: **July 16, 1948**

AIRFRAME

Low unswept wings. Unswept tail surfaces, with dorsal fin and dihedral on tailplane. Conventional control surfaces and double-slotted flaps. Tricycle undercarriage, with twin wheels on each unit. All units retract forward, main wheels into inner engine nacelles.

ENGINES

(Viscount 810). Four Rolls-Royce Dart Mk. 525 turboprops, each rated at 1,990 h.p. and driving a four-blade reversible-pitch airscrew. Fuel tanks in wings, with capacity of 1,900 gal., can be supplemented by two leading-edge slipper tanks with total capacity of 290 gal.

PAYLOAD

Crew of two on flight deck. Seats for up to 73 passengers in pressurised cabin, with toilets, cloakroom, galley and underfloor baggage and freight holds with capacity of 250 cu. ft.

DIMENSIONS

(Viscount 810). *Wing span:* 93′ 8½″.
Length: 85′ 8″.
Height: 26′ 9″. *Wing area:* 963 sq. ft.

WEIGHTS

(Viscount 810). *Empty:* 41,565 lb.
Max. take-off weight: 72,500 lb.

PERFORMANCE

Service ceiling: 25,000′.
Take-off run: 5,930′.
Typical range: 1,725 miles at 355 m.p.h. at 18,000′ with full payload.

Most successful British airliner ever built, the Viscount remained in production for fourteen years and a total of 444 were completed. When the prototype flew in 1948, it was the world's first turboprop transport, yet its testing proved particularly trouble-free. At that time, it was a 32-passenger aircraft, powered by two 1,380 h.p. Dart 502s : but it was clear that the Dart would soon become much more powerful and the Series 700 version ordered into production for B.E.A. in 1950 was a 47-seater with 1,540 h.p. Dart 505s. When the 1,740 h.p. Dart 510 became available in 1956, the opportunity was taken to 'stretch' the Viscount's fuselage by 3 ft. 10 in., making room for 53–65 passengers. The new version was designated Viscount 800 Series and was later followed by the 810 Series, described above, with Darts of still greater power.

VICKERS VANGUARD (Great Britain)

First Flight: **January 20, 1959**

AIRFRAME

Low-mid unswept wings. Unswept tail surfaces, with small dorsal fin and dihedral on tailplane. Conventional control surfaces and Fowler flaps. Tricycle undercarriage, with twin wheels on each unit. All units retract forward, main wheels into inner engine nacelles.

ENGINES

Four Rolls-Royce Tyne Mk. 506 turboprops, each rated at 4,985 h.p. (Vanguard Types 951 and 953) or Tyne Mk. 512 turboprops, each rated at 5,545 h.p. (Type 952). Four-blade reversible-pitch airscrews. Fuel tanks in wings, with capacity of 5,130 gal.

PAYLOAD

Crew of two or three on flight deck. Seats in pressurised fuselage for up to 139 passengers. Two pantries, toilets, wardrobes, and underfloor holds for 1,360 cu. ft. of baggage and freight.

DIMENSIONS

Wing span: 118' 7". *Length:* 122' 10½". *Height:* 34' 11". *Wing area:* 1,529 sq. ft.

WEIGHTS

(Type 952). *Basic operating weight:* 82,500 lb.
Max. take-off weight: 146,500 lb.

PERFORMANCE

(Type 952). *Max. cruising speed:* 425 m.p.h.
Service ceiling: 30,000'.
Typical range: 1,830 miles at 420 m.p.h. at 25,000' with full payload.

Vickers hoped to repeat the success of the Viscount with the larger Vanguard. Unfortunately, by the time it became available for service most airlines had decided to go for jets rather than turboprop aircraft when re-equipping. As a result, sales were limited to six Type 951 and 14 Type 953 Vanguards for B.E.A. and 23 Type 952 Vanguards for Air Canada. The first of the B.E.A. machines entered regular service on March 1, 1961, exactly one month after the first Air Canada Vanguard service was flown. In 1970, B.E.A. had begun converting nine of its Vanguards into Merchantman freighters, with large cargo doors. The Air Canada aircraft are being sold to other airlines, including Angkasa Air Transport of Indonesia.

YAKOVLEV Yak–40 (Russia)

First Flight: **October 21, 1966**

AIRFRAME

Low unswept wings. Sweptback vertical tail surfaces, with variable-incidence tailplane mounted at tip of fin. Conventional control surfaces and simple trailing-edge flaps. Two engines mounted in pods on sides of rear fuselage. Air intake for third engine at base of fin. Tricycle undercarriage, with single wheel on each unit. Nose-wheel retracts forward, main units inward.

ENGINES

Three Ivchenko AI–25 turbofans, each rated at 3,300 lb.s.t. Fuel tanks in wings, with total capacity of 860 gal.

PAYLOAD

Crew of two on flight deck. Pressurised main cabin normally seats 24 passengers three-abreast, but can be fitted with 33 seats in high-density version. All seats can be folded back against the side walls to permit use of aircraft as freighter. Executive versions provide de luxe accommodation for 8–10 persons. Standard Yak-40 has baggage compartment, toilet and wardrobe aft of main cabin. Entry is via an airstair door which forms the underside of the rear fuselage in flight.

DIMENSIONS

Wing span: 82′ 0¼″.   *Length:* 66′ 9½″.
Height: 21′ 4″.   *Wing area:* 753 sq. ft.

WEIGHTS

Basic operating weight: 20,600 lb.
Max. take-off weight: 30,200 lb.

PERFORMANCE

Max. speed: 373 m.p.h.
Take-off run: 1,115–1,180′.
Typical range: 920 miles at 310 m.p.h. with max. fuel.

The idea of using three turbofans in such a small aeroplane may seem strange, but it enables the Yak–40 to operate safely from very short runways. As a result, it is rapidly replacing Russian-built DC-3s (Li–2s) on thousands of short routes in the Soviet Union. Passenger flights with Aeroflot began in September 1968, less than two years after the first flight of the prototype, and the Yak–40 has already found favour outside the Soviet bloc, having been ordered by the Italian airline Air-Tirrena and Lineas Aereas La Urraca of Colombia.

INDEX